THE GATE OF PARADISE
Secrets of Andean Shamanism

Luis Espinoza Chamalú

Translated by
Hilary Dyke

GATEWAY BOOKS
Bath, U.K.

First published 1991 in Spanish under the title
JANAJPACHA – Los Secretos del Chamanismo Andino
Luis Espinoza (Chamalú)
by Ediciones Obelisco, Barcelona

First English Language edition:
© Gateway Books 1998

Published 1998 by
GATEWAY BOOKS
The Hollies, Wellow,
Bath, BA2 8QJ, U.K.

Distributed in the USA by
ACCESS PUBLISHERS NETWORK
6893 Sullivan Road,
Grawn, MI 49637

Translated by Hilary Dyke

Cover Photograph: Kevin Redpath
All photographs © Kevin Redpath except where stated

Set in 10.5pt on 14.5pt Latin, by
Character Graphics (Taunton) Ltd.
Printed by Redwood Books of Trowbridge.

British Library Cataloguing-in Publication Data:
A catalogue record for this book is
available from the British Library

ISBN: 1 85860 043 X

Contents

	Introduction	1
1	These teachings must not remain secret	5
2	Shamanism is not just optimism	49
3	And the Elders told...	77
4	The Cosmic Vision of the Andean Shamans	129
5	A Quechuan Prayer	151
	Glossary	152

Dedication

To Wara, my shining companion, to Dina, the intuitive therapist, to Lara, for her tremendous ability to give to others, to Perico, the embodiment of therapeutic humour, to so many genuine human beings who, despite the tempest of circumstance, are aboard the canoe of growth: Doris, Nelson, Maria Luisa, Honorat, Pili, Mari Carmen, Miguel, Carmen, Joaquin, Chema, Mayte, Creu and Josep; Josep Maria, Eduardo, Manolo, Jos, Luis, Julia, Anita, Jos, Manuel, Angeles, Montse, Nuria, Mariano Bueno, Jaimito, Tomas, Rafael, Waltraud, Choni, Cristina, Maria, Pedro, Maria Rosa, Elena and so many other wonderful pupils, with whom we wrote transcendental, experiential pages, unforgettable episodes, cherished in the most beautiful chapter of our memories.

To the Bibiloni family in Paris, who made us feel at home, to Dr. Carlos Frigola, the conflux of wisdom and science, to Anita Hankoc, with thanks for her friendship, wonderful and wise, to Miguel Blanco and his unforgettable 'Blank Space'. To my mother who, though not understanding what I was doing, always believed in me amid tears and questions; to the Telleria family from Cochabamba, for their unceasing support, and with special affection for my native brothers of the Andes, the Amazon region and the whole wide world.

Thank you for being a real constellation of dreams in constant experiential recreation.

Prologue

When Luis Espinoza, or Chamalú, asked me to write a few lines by way of a prologue to this book, I felt utterly surprised and highly honoured. I thought that this was asked only of very important people and that I should not accept.

He insisted, however, and it seemed to me that there would never be a better opportunity to thank him publicly for his altruistic devotion to others and the deep knowledge which he gleaned from his forefathers over those long years of intense inner toil and sacrifice so as to share it with all of us, in that humble, simple manner which is so typical of him.

As Chamalú says somewhere in this work: "This is not a book; it is an invitation to life".

Yes, my friend, it is an invitation to approach life in a simple, different way, through the wonderfully innocent, shamanic, human focus which invites us to discover life, our life, in its most far-reaching essence.

His verse and his prose, born of a humble, loving heart, can awaken you to the new dawn that you have been waiting to see, a different, simple way of conceiving your existence. As you move through the pages with your heart, you will begin to realise that the shamanic way of life is not reserved for just a few; that permanent contact with your inner shaman will, in a simple way, help you release the great potential within you and that it is only the frontiers of your own making that are fencing it in.

My experience as a therapist has enabled me to see, beyond any doubt, that indeed it is true that the natural state of the human being is one of health and happiness and that the only people who find it are those who are bold and daring enough to throw themselves into life and accept their own selves as creative inhabitants of the planet, with every right to feel well for no particular reason, to live in close proximity to their very selves, integrated through love into their own essence.

So then, each sentence, each paragraph of this book is an invitation to you, to initiate once and for all in the way to be your own therapist, your own master.

Spread the wings of your heart and start flying now towards that wonderful encounter with the Secrets of Andean Shamanism and, without further ado, find your way to *Janajpacha* while never losing sight of your own reality.

Thank you, Luis, in the name of all those people who, like me, will feel understood as they read this book and will know, now and always, that they are never alone, that the heart of the *Pachamama* is boundless and beats in time with our own.

The *Pachamama* will take care of us!

Thank you, *Pachamama*... Thank you.

Dina Garcia
Holistic Therapist (Gerona).

The mountain of Putucusi, Machu Picchu, Peru

Introduction

I was told that the old man had died many years before but that he was, nonetheless, close to me, on his inaccessible mountain, when the treetops awoke in the misty forest.

From the village where he had lived, he came forth one day at dusk. For one hundred years in the village and for thirty in the mountains had he lived and, true to tradition, he allowed us to approach him one day.

This is the setting for our journey towards Andean shamanism. It is the route of *Intij Inti*, of the Path of the Sun, where you will find trees giving advice and rivers ready to listen, mountains offering protection and stars for company, where everything is clothed in the most surprising naturalness, an innocent clarity enabling adults and children alike to take part in a ritual which has become a constantly improving experiential sequence.

This is not just another book; it is a millenary testimony. It is a seed in search of a furrow in your life. It is knowledge stemming from ancient experience, in pursuit of consciences to tune into this experiential frequency. Having sailed adrift from recent history, it is here not only to make you see the lyrical side of your existence but essentially to summon you to a different life. We are not interested in signing manifestoes or attending much-publicised congresses, where money is spent which elsewhere would be enough to feed a child who cannot understand why, once again, he must go to sleep with an empty stomach.

And now, in the absence of words, let this be the call to a full, powerful life, to a reminder that we still have a chance to grow, to be reconciled to the art of living and to gather, beyond the realm of words, like molecules of water in the clouds, forming a galaxy of intentions, a conflux of hearts to build a bridge between the sky and the earth, complete with its own vibrations.

It is not a question of going to a specific place but of galvanising your existence by letting the caterpillar make way for the butterfly, releasing it to fly way up to the pinnacle of freedom.

We have travelled round four continents and spent days on end on motionless mountains; we have given lectures and organised experiential courses, crossed forests and flown over seas. We have travelled without moving and we have moved without travelling; we have wandered within and without until we discovered that 'inside' and 'outside' are two terms which lead to the same point. And here we are in the name of our brothers, raising the timeless voice, making sure that our presence is known, preparing ourselves, with you as well, if you wish, for a life which as yet does not exist but is being engendered as a foretaste in many hearts.

May *Janajpacha* be that point of encounter, the nexus, the bridge, amid the mystic wisdom of the Andes as it slowly starts to appear in the Andes of your heart.

Luis Espinoza (Chamalú)

Outer courtyard, Temple of Kalasasaya, Tiwanaku, Bolivia

CHAPTER ONE

These teachings must not remain secret

Andean shamanism is an art. Become the artist of the supreme art of living, the wayfarer on the sacred way, that being who proceeds relentlessly towards the conquest of his mountain top. The wayfarer is aware of the uselessness of complaining and of the usefulness of problems which, once converted into challenges or trials, strengthen you and show you the way to go. The objects of power are but an extension of inner power, a branch of supreme power.

Once or twice a year, those who live shamanically make the Sacred Pilgrimage to the mountains; it is the pilgrimage of purification, of liberation. At the start of the pilgrimage, the burden is heavy, but the summit is reached with no load at all, with the discovery that all that is necessary is within you. He who returns from the Sacred Pilgrimage is no longer the same. Shamanic power lives on the mountain top. Arise early, bathe in the light of Venus, dance until the rebirth of the *Tata Inti*; then plunge into the river or the sea and be reborn at the same time.

Our shamans are completely cut off in the inaccessible mountains while remaining in contact with the inner shaman of anybody who, in a sincere search, opens his heart to the Universe. To bring shamanism into our lives and into society as a whole is the most natural alternative with which to fight against the alienation and cultural colonisation of our peoples. On seeing our work, some people claim that they can see nothing. In Andean shamanism, there is a visible, explicable level and an invisible one which lies beyond words. You must learn the shamanic art and life will turn into a wonderful adventure.

Instead of letting your inner fire go out, fan it with each thought and act until it takes the form of the glowing star which we used to be before descending to earth. We are proposing that you become a walker on the Path of the Sun. We are proposing that you take the road to lucidity. Sing the magic songs at dawn, at night-time, when you travel and when you come up against adversity. They are the songs sung by the trees at daybreak, in unison with the stars.

Do not be surprised, brother, to find that, in shamanic practices, the drum comes alive and you, in turn, become the drum. There are people who know all our teachings theoretically and accept them intellectually, living their entire lives in a dichotomy which causes them to confuse their dreams with illumination. There are people who, in the name of meditation, prefer to face the boundless challenge of thoughts as onlookers. Our teaching focuses on the perspective of assuming a permanent shamanic attitude in our lives. This is possible from the instant you attain a firm connection with the *Pachamama*.

In the southern Andes, tradition has it that it is woman's sacred mission to awake man, to free him from the dictatorship of his reason so that he may begin to feel. Woman can do this more adeptly when she has not been seduced by comfort, frivolity and stupidity. Once awake and on the same wavelength, a man and a woman are something more than just two people.

We come from the gods and none of us has been assigned the mission of suffering or destruction; none of us has been told: "Go to the Earth and suffer, be distressed; despair, poison yourself, consume until, sooner rather than later, you yourself are consumed by the very thing you've consumed." We come from the stars, in the sense that we are the brightly shining beings we used to be. The stars are there, night after night, to remind us of the way. To be well, we need to be purified, the best way to be purified is to be well, come what may.

When I have a question that needs a quick answer, I tune into my tree and, without further ado, a voice and an image show me the way to go. According to the teachings of the Amautas, the inner garden, the way in to the other reality, is to be found within the *Pachamama*. The passport to the inner garden is humility and absolute silence is the way.

Come and join the *Chej-Pacha* and vibrate in unison with the Universe. Then repose will form part of your labours and the power flowing from you will be present in all you do. Discover the supreme art of living: this means vibrating harmoniously or, in other words, returning to our natural state of, amongst other things, happiness and health. The supreme art of living means a full life which, without taking us from the world in which we live, enables us to live in our own light, invulnerable and steady, where example is our best argument and our presence, even silent, a sufficient contribution.

When you find your centre in the Universe, your place in the *Pachamama*, you will discover that a deep feeling of wellbeing will remain within you whatever may happen. We have only one place. When we fail to occupy it, our actions are bereft of power and so we achieve nothing, no matter how busy we are.

Look for your place and, when you find it, you will change into that invulnerable wayfarer who will discover that the goal is contained in each step and that the instant is only an alias for eternity. When the train of your life starts rolling along the tracks of coherence, the doors of inner power will open at your feet.

The wayfarer does not concern himself with things he does not understand. He feels no distress about past mistakes, nor does he allow himself to be overcome by a fear of the future. The wayfarer is not afraid of going wrong, of striving or of not being understood. He knows that we are here to experiment, to learn and to be permanently available for life. The wayfarer knows that life is a sacred path staking a claim on his steps; that to live is to move forward instead of standing on the side watching; and that the only way to move on is to throw himself fully into each experiential sequence that awaits him.

To remain calm when everyone else loses his nerve is the greatest contribution you can make to others; to be cool-headed when a storm is raging is to act like the channel through which the *Intij Inti* will cast its rays of light, clearing away the blackest darkness.

We are making new furrows with the plough of our ancestors; making furrows for the seed of transcendental Andean knowledge to sprout, grow and blossom. As each day comes, the *Tata-Inti* presents its awe-inspiring auroral show, that precious, glowing instant which will be in vain if the doors of your heart are closed. The wayfarer knows that, as long as we do not allow ourselves to be overcome by failure or a fall, these events turn into the driving force needed to continue and galvanise the climb, interrupted for a split second.

Before progress took the place of life and civilisation gave us a good education, to which many of us in this part of the world have fallen victim; before degeneracy ousted innocence and non-humanity took root with impunity in once-human hearts; before frivolity, the broken vision and the synthetic cult appeared; before ecocide covered the Earth and hearts were eroded, before all that, everything was magical, everything was alive and we were able to talk to the plants and play with the stars, lie back in the arms of the breeze and enjoy the succour of the rivers.

Shamanic experiences are the unquestionable proof of the power and dominion exercised upon the material level by the mind and the subtle. Once the shamanic attitude is brought into your life, you will open your heart and start to tune into the *Pachamama*, becoming a channel of cosmic energy, a being capable, among other things, of performing incredible healings.

Titicaca, the sacred lake where the Incario (the political and social structure of the Inca Empire) was created, is the home of the Inca *ajayús*. There, periodic encounters take place between chosen *yatiris* and shamans; there stands one of the borders between this and the other reality, the invisible door through which we can approach the other reality with greatest ease.

Our children know that animals talk, that the trees and the river offer advice, that the mountain provides shelter and that, when a good man turns into a condor, he takes flight. Our children, those belonging to non-alienated families, have been neither repressed nor tamed; they have not learned to feel embarrassed about their bodies or to deceive themselves. They have learned that life is a game and, if you play it, you will discover that humour is the only serious matter in life.

Our grandparents tell us that the *Lari-lari*, a tiny night bird, may appear in various forms: when a person is sleepy and his eyelids are about to drop, this little bird perches on his heart and steals his *ajayú*; it is every individual's duty to remain on the alert and in a state of wakefulness, chewing coca leaves and thus communing with the vegetable world.

9

The Island of the Sun, Lake Titicaca, Bolivia

It was also told by our grandparents that sucking balls of coca leaf as you sit in a circle and watch the centre of a burning fire enables you to travel to the future that comes before the past and, when you are ready, unsuspected truths are made known to you.

You are at a good level of knowledge when you discover that everything is important, but that nothing is too important; that life is at once a sacred and a breathtaking adventure; that we must assimilate it with humour and with love, with imagination and without fear; that life is to be lived without complicating matters or forgetting its transcendental dimension; that nobody has been assigned any mission other than that of living without more ado.

In no case must the use of magic plants be an end in itself; in most, it may be substituted to advantage by Andean music, the hallucinogen of sound; by dance or by the sequence of solitude, fasting and silence in a cave or on a mountain. Nobody, however, should become fanatical about it, as that would be tantamount to running blindfold along the edge of a yawning abyss. All forms of fanaticism lead us down the road to nowhere. Hallucinogenic plants may or may not be used, depending on the person, the circumstance and the context of the operation. Nothing is indispensable; a profound state of ecstasy may be reached simply by walking on a mountain or dancing at dawn with one's eyes looking East or by blowing a *zanca*.

The mountains taught us to play the pan-pipe. The sound made by this instrument symbolises the breath of the *Pachamama*, the Wayra, as he walks on the meditative mountain. Through the sound of the pan-pipe, the mountain and the wind show us the path of absolute silence as you match breathing to sound and shift into the sound itself, a bridge of sound to the other reality.

If, before building a house, you talk to the land; if, on building it, you strike up a connection with the stones and then wedge them

11

into one another, the result is a wall of energy; and, if the building is circular, an extremely healthy, energising micro-environment is produced. This is the way our forefathers used to build and, while Western temples and convents tumbled to the ground with each seismic tremor, our sanctuaries stood firm. Later, they were taken down and used as quarries by people who saw in them nothing more than a heap of stones.

According to the Incas, a person's health is most clearly expressed in his feet. The feet are virtually the most important part of the body. The Inca enthronement did not consist of placing a crown on the head, but of putting gold sandals on the feet. Tradition has it that the feet are of the utmost importance, not only because they are the mirror of one's health, but also because they enable us to make our way along the very path which is calling for our steps. Life is a path which both demands and attracts the attention of the determined wayfarer.

We do not play music only because it is pleasant, but because essentially, in making music, we are transported to the place where we long to be, beyond time and distance.

Our baptism consists of burying the placenta at the foot of a tree, along with a stone or a flower, as soon as the child is born. The tree protects it, the earth shows it the *Chej-Pacha*, the stone endows it with a will of rock and the flower gives sweetness, gentleness and inner beauty. This baptism will last until the end of infancy, when the child shall either renew it by undergoing the shamanic initiation trials or turn his back on the *Pachamama* with no aim other than to be prematurely consumed by the very thing he has consumed. The *Pachamama* does not condemn; the paths are similar to one another but they do not all lead to life.

Ritual is the bridge that links us to the other reality. If, however, it is performed outside its sacred context, it lacks power and meaning.

One day, a species similar to the human being stepped out of the sea. Their skin was so pale that it was as if the *Tata Inti* had declined to look upon them. They covered their bodies with tough leaves and, as they spoke, they spat fire. They seized the sacred objects, destroyed our magic places, slashed our roots and poured scorn on the elders and the forefathers.

Despite having played a part in recent history by laying the dead to rest, despite all that, we are here today, sharing the teachings of the invisible book of our ancestors, in the hope that our presence will be a gesture of fraternity from our hearts to yours. Our forefathers expressed themselves basically through symbols. That is why those born of a different culture understood little or nothing when they tried to get an insight into ours.

The dimension of the sacred will become meaningful in your life when you stop considering only the visible as real. The invisible is the most important; the essential is not visible to the eye, but to the heart. We are perpetuating creation in its most beautiful sense. Those amongst our people who have not been debased, our brothers all over the world, are the living example of the fact that living can be different.

And here we are to remind you that the time to live is still not over, that to live in ecological awareness is a matter of urgency, that the *Pachamama* awaits us with open arms, that it is possible to relate to it and all the protection it offers. Our people have still not learned to grow bored, or to make life difficult for themselves or to spend all their time thinking, only to think that one should not think.

We have not learned to use a knife and fork; we know only how to enjoy what we eat, however meagre the food may be; we have not learned to lie or to deceive. What we do know is that our ancestors and many of us today have been the victims of those who have learned the art of deceit and practise this repugnant profession.

We have not learned to walk quickly, because when we start running we stop enjoying the journey and no longer feel the living presence of the *Pachamama* caressing our feet at each step; nor can we eat quickly because our sisters, the plants and the trees, feel angry when we do not respect their work; when we take food disrespectfully, then we eat in vain.

We have not understood what private property is. We do not understand how it can be that something is for one person only and for nobody else, when the *Pachamama* has taught us that all is for all: the air that brings us together, the rivers that wash our problems away, the mountain that reminds us of the attitude towards life, the *Tata Inti*, evoking within us the importance of lucidity, the stars reminding us of the path to take.

We have not yet learned to say one thing and do another, to give a nod of the head, but not of the heart, to think that we know it all. We do not know many things, we just want to live; we are not specialists in any field, we just want to live, to live with reverence and without fear, to live in love with life, hand in hand with the *Pachamama* and to leave a home for our children like the one left to us by our forebears.

Many of us have still not learned to read and write; we know only how to read the message written in invisible ink on each leaf, on each flower, each dawn. We have not learned to give ourselves titles, we love our names and we are happy simply to be human beings. We cannot live without sharing what we have and we are grateful to anyone who lets us give him something.

We are simple, like the breeze as it plays with the flowers when the twilight comes; we are born of our land, a land that walks, *Pachamama* dressed as man and woman, a humanised plot of the Universe. We are the children of humanity, we continue to embody innocence, spontaneity, naturalness. We know that we are neither better nor worse, just different; we have learned to walk the world clad in sincerity, free of inferiority and superiority complexes, fears and arrogance.

Life is a ritual in which each act and thought acquires fundamental importance and come to life; where every single fact and intention related to the *Pachamama* shift ever-increasing energy forces. Life is the ritual of access to light. The reason is to be found on a narrow path which must be abandoned so as to gain access to the wide avenues of feeling. This is when you will discover that the visible is the least important, that you are far more than what is seen by the naked eye. When that time comes, you will be able to avail yourself immediately of cosmic energy as you will have merged into *Pachamama*.

When past invaders met our forefathers, they were surprised at the moral and ethical level in our country. Our forefathers refused to lie and deceive, to steal and destroy the *Pachamama* and, essentially, to lie to themselves. When they were led to the gallows or the stake, they were aware that, through death, they were just being reallocated in the cosmos in a different manner. Our mystical-spiritual tendency is spontaneous and forms part of the natural condition of the human being and now, perhaps more so, of our people in particular, recipients of the invisible, the vital space where earthly and cosmic energies converge and do not go unnoticed.

Although our communities were ostracised and destroyed, not a finger was laid upon the invisible communities, the fundamental trustees of essential knowledge, swathed for so long in the utmost secrecy which only now is being revealed, coinciding in time with the completion of one *Pachacuti* (cycle) and the advent of another. According to tradition, whenever a *Pachacuti* is completed, everything turns the other way round: what was considered as true proves to be false and what was known as superstition turns out to be the truth. A *Pachacuti* has been completed.

Our therapy is based not only on the visible. Our life is much more than what can actually be seen. It is the invisible that matters. We have a sacred duty: to live, to live with no complications, seduced by abundance. We are alive only when we are growing. To live is to embody the supreme art of growing.

By dancing, you can make contact with trees and animals; by relating to them and acquiring their attributes, you will discover that time and distance do not exist, that many things that are false in this reality are true in the other. Evolve into the artist of the sacred. Alter your life into a wonderful work of art. You are an experiential poem. Sacred accounts make a transparent link between this reality and the other. Ritual provides the context, like the furrow that opens the way for the seed of power to sprout.

After the initiation ceremony in the magic grotto, the initiated's body is covered in lantin, a radiant wrapping, that strange glow surrounding the body, remaining with whoever possesses it from then on. The rainbow is the supreme stairway to the *Janajpacha*, showing that, though the ways are many, the perspective is the same, that we need not concern ourselves with the colour of our path but just make sure that we are on our way and are gaining ground.

Some people are travelling down the wrong path, which is tantamount to fighting in the enemy's trench. Make sure that you are moving along the rainbow, the fail-safe route to the *Janajpacha*. Grow like the trees, always reaching upwards and never losing sight of this reality: it is also necessary to be here and make a contribution through our constructive example.

Sacred places are to be found in the thick forest, in the depths of the cavern, on the mountain top, from where it proves easier to approach the other reality, providing that the suitable ritual setting is there. The principal sacred place, however, is in your heart. Unless you go first to your heart, it is impossible for you to go anywhere. It is like acting as a volcano, whose fire and heat are released to the outside world. Let that immense power within you be released. Once that happens, your life will have begun.

Andean shamanism is the cosmic religion, the experiential philosophy, poeticised existence. Andean shamanism is the sacred art of transforming the invisible into the visible, of building a life of transcendental dimensions with each act and intention.

At the Andean shamanism initiation ceremony the aspirant sees the night Sun and, from that moment onwards, he never walks in darkness again. Anybody who approaches the *Pachamama* with sincerity can live in a state of enlightenment. Initiate your steps on the sacred path of life.

The Andean condor is the symbol of the visionary journey, of the ecstatic flight, of access to *Janajpacha*. The condor does not fear earthly commotions, because he knows that he can soar way above them and reach the pinnacle of invulnerability. You are a condor.

You want to know if we can see God? Of course we can see him! Disguised as a tree, a mountain, a river, a flower or a star. Even a child's smile or the silence of a victim of discrimination is the presence of God camouflaged. Come and discover your wings. You are a condor, start to fly, soar high above where meanness and frivolity cannot reach, where all that counts is essence, not insignificance. Fly, up and up until your wings caress the pure air of wisdom, cleansed of all erudition; perch on the branches of the cosmic tree. Today, as yesterday, it awaits your arrival.

Manco Kapac and Mama Ocllo, the founders of the political and social structure of the Inca Empire (Incario), are pictured always surrounded by animals, some of them wild. Whenever they went to the country, their presence was a source of argument. "No animal

Pachamamma

ever attacks a human being", they said, "when he is in harmony and contact with the *Pachamama*."

The *Illapa* (beam or ray) is the stairway of light which joins the sky to the earth. The *Illapa* reminds the determined wayfarer on the sacred path that his way will turn into light when, despite all trials and tribulations, he marches on with perseverance.

For the native people of the Andes, this is also a cardinal point, the standpoint, as each person is a different possibility of the same thing. The perceptive quality is of great importance because your standpoint is the door through which you gain access to reality. A false door leads to the approximation of illusion, of the dream that will replace the awakening. If there are flaws in your standpoint, in the way in which you perceive yourself and discern in general, then it is likely that your priorities and your guiding star flawed.

One of the elders used to say: I am also a jaguar, a condor, a butterfly, a tree, a mountain, a river, a star, light, silence, a vacuum; all and nothing, but not in this reality. There are things that are untrue in this reality and are true in the other, which also exists.

Days of fasting before the sequence of dances, silence and solitude, prior to the music and the social gathering, facing the invisible so as later to spin the web of experiential sequences, at once an inner and an outer task, finding the meditative dimension of each activity: this was our life and so it is when we are allowed to live.

The sacred fire burning in your inner self waxes with each act of love and wanes when your actions are driven by selfishness, frivolity and wickedness. The sacred fire is the remains of the star you were once, the memento of the bright perspective you are to pursue until the day comes when you reach the pinnacle of your mountain and clothe yourself in light, becoming a star once more. In our temples and on our monoliths, the figure of a winged man can be seen, a symbolic allusion to the shamanic flight, the visionary journey far beyond time which revives or overtakes events. It is not impossible to fly once we refuse to believe that only what we see is real. There is nothing newer than ancestral knowledge and nothing older than the techniques and teachings of the New Age. The old novelties are starting to emerge, the essence is the same, the clothing is of no interest. It is something that lies beyond time and space.

Shamanic therapy is integral, concerning a way of perceiving and thinking, of living and forming relationships, of nourishment and work. It includes specific preparations for local use, solar, stellar and earthly energising agents, visualisation, harmonisation with the *Pachamama* and the transfer to the latter of problems and ailments, once the message contained has been understood. Shamanic therapy is an invitation to a life with power and a multi-dimensional connection; it is the journey into your depths and the discovery that the inside and the outside are, at bottom, one and the same thing.

Uwaro Khocha is the son of the *Tata Inti*, the fully-fledged wayfarer who never stops and never turns off the path, but moves on, invulnerable, his entire route melting into a pattern to be followed. Uwaro Khocha marches on relentlessly because he does not cling on to anything, not even the outcome of his actions or life, because he knows that this is not the way to life, that it is life itself and that, by living to the full, we discover the invisible goal that is present throughout the journey.

Man is the space where the visible and the invisible shake hands. Man is the instant of instinct, where all is possible, even stupidity. Man is the door to heaven, to light and to the option of darkness.

20

Man is the opportunity for all or nothing, for transcendence or frivolity, for abundance or robotisation; man is eternity in the disguise of the temporary, the sacred path on which it is possible even... even to commit a parking offence and speak of life from a standpoint of suicide by installments.

Dressed in transparent white, Uwaro Khocha went from village to village, bearing a message of love and fraternity. He said that we are all brothers, that we must share, that he who has least is he who has most, that we come into the world unfinished for the very purpose of completion, that this is our only task and that it is done by living hand in hand with the *Pachamama*, which stands by every step we take on this pilgrimage to infinity.

Uwaro Khocha was all sweetness and love. Once, when he was teaching in a village that had fallen into the grasp of corruption, he was taken prisoner, punished and tied up on the top of a high mountain so that the birds of prey would come and devour him. However, when the birds saw him, they took food to him. Tradition has it that, having changed into a condor, Uwaro Khocha went flying to the *Janajpacha*, promising to return and revive Andean teachings.

When you open your heart to the cosmos and lie back in the arms of the *Pachamama*, you begin to sense that stones talk, the trees and the river sing beautiful songs, the mountains offer shelter, the flower gives encouragement and the stars show the way to go. Let the *Apu Inti*, the solar essence, light your inner path; let the *Tata Inti* show you, with its birth and its death, your route through this world, reminding you with each dawn that it is never too late to be born again.

When our forebears appeared, animals talked to men. Now they can communicate only with those who are in harmony with the *Pachamama*. In modern times, the city man cannot talk even to other men; many of them cannot live even with their own selves and,

The "El Fraile" stela standing at the south-western corner of the Temple of Kalasasaya, Tiwanaku, Bolivia

avoiding the issue with meaningless prattle, they flee from the silence which would otherwise force them to take a good look at themselves.

The living bewail the death of the departed; the dead shed tears for the living who stayed behind. Which is better, this existential page or the next one?. This one is more important now, the next one is more important later, everything is important – within its own time, nothing is important outside that time.

Like someone revealing the strictest of secrets, one of my countrymen told me in a whisper of his discovery that, in the cities, the doctor, the psychologist and the priest are different people and that, more often than not, they do not agree even among themselves. "They're three different people, and nobody has realised this," said the old man, unable to come to terms with his discovery.

Andean shamanism is simply the way to harmonisation with the *Pachamama*, a wonderful journey in which the supernatural and the esoteric blend into a natural, spontaneous and creative experiential sequence. Modern man will never be able to explain the construction of great temples, monuments and other majestic Andean buildings while he stubbornly insists on using his intellect as an instrument to understand non-intellectual knowledge. To live intellectually is tantamount to going on a hike and walking on only one foot.

Basically, the diverse universe is an indivisible unit; the *Pachamama* is one too, with an assortment of clothing. However, while this supreme unit is invisible to the eye, it is unmistakable to the heart which is open to the cosmic vibration.

We are asked repeatedly about meditation techniques. For us, to live is to meditate, all is meditation, when you set your steps in the right direction. There is no better way than life, nor is there a better wayfarer than the person who is ready for life, rain or shine.

You are *Pachamama*, the forest in which we, the indigenous people of South America, are fighting. You are *Pachamama*, wearing temporary humanised clothes. You are *Pachamama*, you are not alone, the rest of the infinite *Pachamama* is with you.

I sense eternity flowing through my body, the infinite parked on the tracks of my memory. So – what do I have to fear if I am greater than circumstances and my greatness, beating darkness off, turns death into the dawn of another day? I sense that life has an appointment with myself – and I hasten to be present.

My countrymen and I are cosmically free because we have not forsaken the natural condition in which all human beings ought to live; because we have not sacrificed innocence, nor have we given up spontaneity; because we have learned that we do not have to be specialists in anything – except in living. When we lean on the *Pachamama* and settle down in the cosmos, we taste freedom in freedom. When we move away from nature and turn our backs on it, we feel the weight of slavery which, in the form of unhealthy habits and addictions to unnecessary needs and brainwashing, makes life into an insignificant, excruciating existence.

Hark the voice of the *Pachamama* calling from within you! Sense the eloquent silence, the invisible letter from your inner *Pachamama*! Feel, rethink your priorities, change the direction of your march, your path is there, waiting for your steps.

What is life? Life is a sequence of love. Stop living in disarray on the outside and start making contact with the *Pachamama* who will put your pieces together and set you down in the cosmic silence, giving you an inner peace which never again shall be interrupted even when you return to external activities. Stop surviving. It is time to live.

It is absurd to speak of freedom from a pathetic position in some corner of our prison when we have the key to the cell. Some people talk on and on about freedom while the interminable clangour of their own cherished shackles can be heard in the background. Take refuge in the *Pachamama* and you will find that there is nothing to look for, that everything has always been here, waiting to be discovered.

Contact with the *Pachamama* is expressed in the loving presence, an expression of abundance requiring no words in which to clothe it. Where do I live? I live in my heart, a branch of the *Pachamama*. The route traced by the *Pachamama* is wondrous, full of teachings and pleasant surprises, abounding in love and humour; all that is required is that you come along.

If you awake to life, life will awake within you. Full-scale contact with nature is our best nourishment. What we bring is in no way strange; our message is an invitation to life, a proposal for abundance, a return to our natural state – naturally.

The only way to get to know the path is to tread it. Andean shamanism is the Path of the Sun, the route of lucidity. It matters not what you say if your attitude says the opposite. Let your example be the best argument and your presence full and silent, the invisible advice that no one may dispute.

The forest dwellers say that he who is in a bad mood is sick and that he who is sick and does not direct his steps towards health is guilty of a flagrant violation of the *Chej-Pacha*.

The silence to which we invite you is not only verbal, it is mental too. This is the silence of quality, the setting in which your inner power bursts forth and flourishes. Be humble and you will go a long way; be loyal to your own self; you are life. Life is our path, life is our goal. Life is the best technique, a wonderful opportunity to grow in the midst of a sea of circumstance. Life is you and your only task is to grow.

Music is the bridge of sound between the *Chej-Pacha* and the *Janajpacha*, between this reality and the other. Our dances are a journey to our own self and thence to the supreme source of energy, where all is a cosmic dance.

25

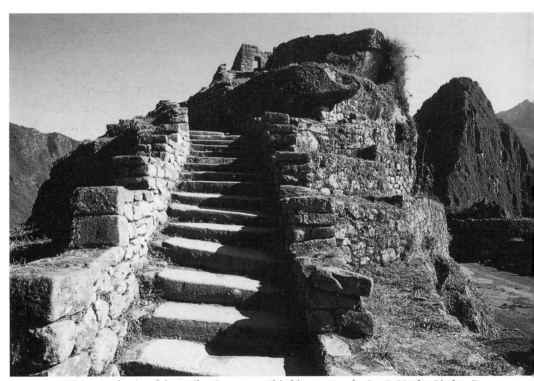

Stairway to the site of the Intihuatana stone "hitching post to the Sun", Machu Picchu, Peru

At our school, people are initiated into life. The most important things are expressed by us in silence. People are discontented with their lives because they have not understood the transcendental reason for their journey through this world. We, the people born of this land, have a special feeling for the transcendental. We try not to mix it up with the pseudo-spiritual rubbish that is using its name to dazzle the mind and to fetter people's existence, when transcendence is, in fact, precisely the road to liberation.

Brother, let the *Pachamama* show itself in you. Andean shamanism is the initiatory ceremony enabling you to enter life with no middlemen or delays. Only when you drink from the fountain will you quench your thirst. There is a range of fountains and a good number of dealers who sell second-hand water sweetened by their own techniques. The thirst of those who drink it is quenched for a time but, sooner or later, thirst returns with a vengeance, always supposing that the drinker has not been poisoned in the process.

When you tune into the *Pachamama*, your problems vanish on the spot; they are taken up, recycled and returned to you in the form of flowers by the *Pachamama*. When man has reached a state of harmony through the Universe, he is unfailingly ready for anything, he senses that everything is possible. Silence is just a different, deeper form of communication. When you have the courage to look beyond your own bounds, you will discover that you have no bounds at all. The guardian spirit makes itself known through intuition when we are not condemned to being slaves of reason.

For the people of the Andes, eating is a sacred matter, a full-blown act of meditation. Eating is sacred because food is the dwelling of the *Intij Inti*, supreme energy in a natural, biodegradable pack. Our essential knowledge is embodied and preserved by invisible men who, disguised as visible beings, make their way silently through this reality. Meditate as you fast in silence, solitude and darkness within this far-reaching context. You will be able to hear the voice of the *Pachamama* and you will have a perfectly clear idea of what you have to do. If nature is more than what the eye can see, you can cope with more than you think you can.

I have travelled across madness like a train crossing a bridge. I have seen microscopic monsters devouring the beautiful and small planet Earth, a delicate creature crying out in agony. I have sensed the weeping of the trees and have felt the cries of pain of rivers and seas; I have felt the despair of whales and the call of the mountains.. And I have returned to live on the threshold of sanity while, out of the corner of my eye, I watch the necrophilic procession called progress go by.

"How could we", said a fellow countryman, "explain to the city dweller the immense beauty of the *Pachamama*, summed up in a star, a flower, a sunset or the morning chorus of the birds? How could we show him that all is one, that everything is alive, that we are the same seed with a different husk? How could we make him see that we are all swathed in the same dawn, the transparent breath of the loving *Pachamama*, who rocks us on the lap of nature in an invisible embrace? How could we show him the everlasting kiss of light given each day by the *Tata Inti* and its nightly invitation to lucidity, issued in chorus with the stars in spite of the darkness?

Could you, city man, could you understand that all is one, that Pachamama is you, that the closest distance between two beings is love, that a drop of rain is the universe in a nutshell and that a well-meant intention is the best gift of powerful vibration?

We of the Andes have vanquished time. We are today, as yesterday, treading the paths of the modern twentieth century, clothed in our magic-ancestral heritage, capable of feeling good for no particular reason. Being alive in the midst of so much beauty is sufficient reason for feeling good. Despite it all, despite recent history, we have not ceased to purify our bodies and free our minds of unharmonious thoughts. Today, city brother, you may look into our eyes and find the transparency of the stream as it reflects the sun. Today, you can hear our voices as they mingle with the warbling of the nightingale and the goldfinch. Birds have taught us to realise that life is a hymn to the *Pachamama*.

Modern man, we are aware that you are also a brother of ours, that we are flowers of the same cosmic tree, that in the depths of our hearts burns the eternal fire we used to be before descending to Earth, the star that we shall become when this journey is over. Modern man, let our voice join the voice that is struggling to escape from the depths of your heart, making its way through thoughts and prohibitions, conditioning factors and trends, habits and routine attitudes; let the voice of your heart take the place of the voice of your head; let your tree blossom. We are aware that we all come from the same seed.

We have been climbing this path for thousands of years; we have seen seductive autumns, whose trees gave up the external to embark on an inner voyage, bare of all superficiality, cleansed of all outer show; we have been through bleak, leafless winters, casually dressed in clouds, finding shelter in the fire of our hearts, sensing that Mother Nature has a pleasant surprise in store for those of us who have understood the message implicit in her cold presence.

And we have forged ahead. We have discovered that, when we persevere, we find strength in adversity; that winter never comes into our hearts and that, when darkness seemed to be at its darkest, a distant star, shimmering behind the darkness, wrapped us in light once more, urging us to carry on; that no darkness can touch our hearts when we are firmly settled in our cosmic dimension.

As we went on our way, we came upon the warm presence of the *Tata Inti*. Clad in the dawn, it helped fend off all the darkness. And the *Pachamama* began to smile through the many-coloured petals and the scented air; spring is a reward for those who persevere. Spring is the awakening, the music after the silence, the certainty that we must press on. What would have happened if we had stayed behind hopelessly in the winter? What would have happened if, by clinging on to the cold, we had missed the spring of existence?

Now, from the spring of our hearts, we can talk to the blossoming tree, to the bird in its cosy nest; now we can sense the arrival of the summer, the instant of eternity when man discovers the supreme brotherhood, weaving a multicultural fraternity in search of diverse unity.

Brother of the city, do not linger in the winter of life; do not allow yourself to be paralysed by the cold or let your feet wander away from the path. The door of *Jatunwasi* remains open, there in the summer of life, where love, in the form of warmth, envelopes your heart until it returns you to the cosmic dimension.

It matters not whether you are now naked or covered in wretchedness, addiction or unwholesome habits; it matters not that frivolity has a hold on you and that meaninglessness has you temporarily in its grasp, that your days go by on the circular tracks of robotic, mechanising routine; it matters not that the flowers in the garden of your heart have faded and that you have hidden your inner vacuum under a pile of external elements. It matters not that, for so long, you have been forgetful of the way and that you have gone off to fight in the wrong trench; it matters not that, as a result of so much thinking, your thoughts have become your own prison and your actions degraded to their basest expression. It matters not that, so as to keep up with appearances, you have lied to yourself and that you have neglected to nurture, enhance and release the huge potential you carried within you; none of this matters if, from within, you wish it to be that way. Very soon, the garden of your heart will abound with flowers again, giving you and your life an everlasting inner spring, preceded by a majestic dawn, returning life to your life. You will live in a state of dawn. Brother, the time to live has come.

We, the people of the Andes, know that when a person dresses in humility, he becomes transparent; that when he wraps himself in silence, he becomes powerful; that when his steps are well-intentioned and come from the heart, each action ripens into a candescent being, like a tree dancing in the morning, like a condor on its initiatory flight, like a star twinkling in its brightness.

We know that we can all become the wayfarer vibrating with each step, a being that does not cling unconditionally on to anything, just as the Sun does not cling to the dawn, or the rain to the clouds. Everybody, including you, Western brother, can come and listen to the music of the stars and join the dance of the trees, meditate with the mountain and stroll with the river, talk to the flowers and disappear with the Brother Wayra, the invisible traveller thanks to whom we are able to listen to silence.

Modern brother, if you are willing to listen, we might tell you that birdsong is a constant reminder that it is still time to live. Modern brother, we would like to tell you a secret: the Earth does not belong to us, but to our ancestors who admired it and to our children who will find shelter there, to the animals and plants that accomplish their evolutionary mission on it. The Earth does not

Family home on The Island of the Sun, Lake Titicaca, Bolivia

belong to us; we just look after it and learn from it at the same time.

Our grandparents tell us that the *Pachamama* used to be far more beautiful when it clad itself in woods and adorned itself with flowers as they played each day with colourful butterflies. Our children used to talk to invisible children, the elders had the benefit of the advice of the trees, the long-lived wise, always ready to guide the pilgrim on his way. Women would comb their long hair, damp from the glistening morning dew falling as they danced and sang in chorus with the birds that would, at one and the same time, strike up their daily symphony of thankfulness for the new day. Men would go out in search of food and wisdom; they sometimes spent the whole day enjoying the lessons written in invisible ink on each leaf, on each drop of rain, each nightfall. Then they would return home with the food, tree-packed energy. It was all quite simple, like a clear brook. Our steps were guided by a secret: the Earth did not belong to us, we were just looking after it!

The grandmother lay sleeping in the street. The grandmother always seemed all right. As she had nothing, not even a place to sleep, passers-by would ask her to explain her wellbeing. She adamantly insisted that she was wealthier than everybody else because she found intense enjoyment in the dawn that met her eyes after she had spent a night in the arms of the cosmos under a huge dark blanket covered in stars. Opening her arms, the grandmother used to say: "All is ours, even the things that our eyes cannot see; all is here to help us, we are not alone, all, absolutely all, is for us." And the grandmother did not feel that she was the owner of anything; she knew that everything was there for her to enjoy it.

"In the past", an elder nostalgically recalled, "things used to be simpler, men did not rush about and women sang to the breeze, a lady in an invisible dress came by our home every day, kissing flowers and caressing hair."

In the past, problems were less of a problem, people did not sink under the strain of stress, nor did they commit suicide or take drugs or deceive themselves. In many communities, things are very much as before. Can it be that we are primitive and have not progressed? Can it be that we are savages because we feel that problems are not a problem in themselves, but hinge upon an approach which frequently leaves a lot to be desired?

We are expected to be Western but, wherever we cast our eyes, we see their system crumble and fall. My brothers, let us change direction! The West is a blind alley.

When you settle down into the liberated zone of your mind, you approach the magic area of life, where everything is love and harmony. The day that no thought strolls through your mind with impunity, you will have reached the oasis where the never-ending spring of wisdom bubbles.

What is life? Life is poetry. What is poetry? Poetry is magic. What is magic? Magic is life, seduced by abundance.

Come and live fully today to be reborn tomorrow, just as the Sun reappears each day, not discouraged by the darkness that came before. Each day is a rebirth as you, sliding into the Sun, embark upon the path of lucidity. As this message flies across the paths of your mind, let it reach your heart. There, the furrows are ready for the seeds of all essential knowledge to grow. Night smiles through the stars, reminding you that, beyond darkness, the light shines again.

There is nothing to discuss, brother. We all come from a common source. If you open your heart, all is one. Inside and out, it is the same. We know that. We, the Andean people, have a covenant with

Couple farming on the Peruvian altiplano

the *Pachamama* who, with silent eloquence, has taught us to live respectfully and tolerantly. No, brother, your message and ours are one and the same gift; it is just that the verbal wrapping is different.

The Amautas claimed that happiness and humour are the yardstick of health. We have no right to be sick with unhappiness or to suffer from the malignant tumour of ill humour.

We, the people of the Andes, are in love with the natural state in which we have always grown. We have given up on civilised Western life, where everything is so well-timed and rehearsed; where we had to make progress instead of living; where our children's creativeness was repressed and their imagination thwarted; where they were trained as would-be penpushers, the democrats of the future tamed into being their own oppressor; where we had to renege on our values and break away from our roots and lower ourselves to the level of robots, dead beings with no appetite, with no aim other than that of consuming synthetic, expensive rubbish. We have learned to abandon anything that goes against life. We want to live. We know, we sense that, despite it all, it is still possible to live.

Our family is made up of men and women, trees and rivers, mountains and rocks, of stars, of the moon and the animals, of the *Tata Inti* and the sacred *Pachamama*. We are at once many and one. And we are all alive.

To be unhappy and to lead a life of misery is to show a lack of respect for the *Intij Inti* and to spurn the sacred teachings. To those who claim to have five senses, we say that they are lacking in one: the sense of the sacred. Without that, man is lost.

He who moves away from the *Pachamama* lives on the edge of stupidity and suicide. He who does not love what he does runs the risk of poisoning himself. Each moment is a well of eternity: it is neither long nor short, it is just an opportunity.

We bring the unmistakable message of the *Tata Inti*, inviting you, in chorus with the stars, to flee from the deadening comings and goings of everyday life; to become a pilgrim of lucidity, to gear your body towards the silent, spontaneous movement of the cosmic dance in which we find ourselves.

We bring a message that will enable you to reinvent your life. If nature is more than what the eye can see, you can embrace more than you think.

They took down our temples to use them as a quarry. Now nothing remains but mere traces. However, the most important temples are to be found in our hearts, whence we begin to come forth with the knowledge they were unable to destroy; a teaching whose purpose is to rebuild the state of consciousness in which we have to live.

The age of the native is coming. It is starting now, clothed in humility, the best way to show essential knowledge. We are all natives when we return to our natural state. He who is not ready to live to the full has already started to die.

There is nothing more magical than a flower, a rainbow, a sunset; nothing more magical than the mist caressing the mountain, the goldfinch greeting the day, the glow-worms imitating the stars. And the West asks us if we believe in magic. We respect nature and nature protects us.

Think? What for? We were told that all we had to do was live!

An indigenous child said: "Why don't the grown-ups of the city play any more? Why do they all look so serious? Who has forbidden them to play and laugh?" The glittering night smiles down through the stars; the *Pachamama* smiles at you through flowers of many colours.

37

Smile! We know that humour is the only serious question.

My tears melt into a tributary of the Amazon whenever, instead of forest, I find an unbearable green desert. My tears and the rain have blended into each other in a nostalgic embrace, reminiscent of what it used to be, trying to moisten the tarmac of indifference and fan each conscience into nurturing the desire to move away from reason towards the heart, from thinking to feeling, from calculating to loving, from speculating to giving, away from the daily destruction of supreme creation.

We, the indigenous people, are all farmers; we tend the fruits of the earth and our lives on the plot of universal existence which we have been destined to plough. Every intention is a word, every action a verse from your own existential poem in this experiential sequence.

The tree said to the pilgrim: all we have to do is grow; there is no task other than that of everlasting growth. If life is a gift, then we accept it gratefully; if it is an opportunity, then we also accept it gratefully. Those who complain are but fools who have understood nothing.

We know that to carry the weight of distress is optional; that things look bad when the message attached to them is missed, and that making life difficult for ourselves is not the task which we have been assigned. When we stop thinking and open our hearts to the *Pachamama*, we sense the music of the stars piping through our bodies in harmony, taking us into the endless cosmic dance that we have all been invited to join.

Do not fear death at a certain stage of your life; give up what once seemed important to you, just as the *Tata Inti* gives up the blue of the sky to be born again the following day in a majestic dawn.

He who has found life has discovered that the night is magic, that the woods are magic, that the rain is magic, that the expression in the eyes of a harmonious person is magic, that magic

38

Young children at Sacsayhuaman, Peru

is the passport to a full life, that magic purifies us and makes our life into a sacred ritual where actions and intentions dance together, holding hands in a coherent symphony, joining gesture to dream, word to experience.

Life becomes magical once we reach an agreement with the *Pachamama*, enabling us to learn from each moment and enjoy it, on that unique journey to the infinite.

No, brother of the West, do not continue down the path of stressful life; do not go on beating your brains out. You cannot spend your entire life on the top of a palm tree. Come down to earth, return to the simple things in life, transcendence wears the clothes of simplicity; in many cases, the complex, the 'super-esoteric', is rubbish disguised as a spiritual message. Come down to life, dress in the robes of humility, admit that you are ignorant: essential knowledge has nothing to do with the intellectual accumulation of facts and figures. Retrace your steps down former paths, stop for a minute, plunge into a vacuum of reflection, the route to your inner world. Forgive yourself; what matters is not what you did or failed to do yesterday but the direction of your steps set once more towards life. As you move along, you will sense all the strength of the *Pachamama* as it is released within you.

What god are we talking about if there is but one with different aliases? How can we search for him if we have not even discovered his visible presence expressed through nature? If you allow yourself to fall into the arms of abundance, you will begin to discover life from its nethermost point. There is a miracle that you are called upon to perform: the miracle of discovering the supreme art of living. You ask me who I am. I am a tree clad as a human being. I am a travelling tree.

Only the wayfarer is shown the way by the *Pachamama*. He who stays behind remains in darkness.

If you go through life giving away honest smiles irrespective of circumstances; if you keep calm when everybody else panics; if you struggle without clinging on to the outcome; if you love cosmically, in exchange for nothing; if you dress in the clothes of humility, then you embody life in its most beautiful expression and stand as a forerunner of the New Humanity.

Stop treading the shores of ignorance; have the courage to approach the delicate vessel that will cross the restless, stormy river and lead you to the shores of wisdom. Remember that living means throwing oneself into life instead of standing on the shore like a chicken that refuses to hatch.

It is not possible to build a new world without saying goodbye to old forms of perception and life; it is not possible to become part of the New Humanity without opening up to the *Pachamama* and settling down in the cosmos, without vibrating in tune with the Universe. Let cosmic energy flow through you, changing you into a channel of supreme wisdom. When that happens, the creative power of the *Pachamama* will flow within you, like the light of a star or the water of a spring.

When we are in touch with the *Pachamama*, our path is bright. The *Pachamama* appears in many ways and intuition is one of them. When you are at peace with the *Pachamama*, then all is at peace and your presence, even when silent, is a fraternal gesture of peace.

Search for your cosmic and your comic dimension. Nothing is too important, everything has its importance. Humour is the only serious matter in life. When you are alone with the *Pachamama*, its secrets will be entrusted to you in a silent language, in a message invisible to your eyes. With your actions and thoughts, you bring happiness or sadness to your life. There is nothing decided that your own decision cannot alter. Recreate each day of your life, like the Sun as it shows you the way with each dawn.

The teachings of the *Pachamama* expressed in Andean shamanism are hard: there are no lies, nor are you allowed to go on deceiving yourself. The *Pachamama* places a mirror before you, where you can see all the rubbish that you have been carrying inside yourself. The *Pachamama* forces you to be practical and demands coherence of you. It is in this setting that inner power and innocence show through.

If your way is not carpeted with flowers, do not complain: it is there that the charm of life lies. To grow and to blossom, it is necessary to die. Plastic flowers, ignorant of the darkness and harshness of the soil, have no life. Brother, your way is carpeted with flowers – beyond the early stones and pains. Let the light of the stars hold sway over your darkness. Wear the clothes of transparent light that the stars have designed for those who take the path to the Sun.

At the schools of modern man, it is taught that human beings have only five senses. This is true only of those who are imprisoned by the walls of pathetic frivolity. These reduce man to a mere visible context which, in actual fact, is of the least importance.

No, Andean shamanism is not a panacea. It is a millenary experience which, in the form of testimonies, evolves into a way of life, capable of providing keys and clues with which to solve the full range of contemporary problems. We are offering you a shamanism which is accessible to all, without being broken off from its essence.

Andean shamanism is a reminder that it is better to live in light. Our forefathers taught us that the gods revealed their secrets to the trees. The Amautas said that he who lives with no inner growth lapses into slavery. We are wandering stars on the route to the infinite, bound for eternity. Let not your mind be the tomb of your spirit or your thoughts the prison of your heart.

The sacred planet Earth is not the right home for those who persist in confusing their dreams with transcendental reality, denying its multi-dimensional nature and existence clothed in eternity. The *Pachamama* is not for those who have chosen destruction and ignorance instead of growth and who neither enjoy its presence nor understand its way.

Shamanism teaches you a different way of seeing things and, accordingly, a different way of living your life. No frontier is the last, no border is final. Forge ahead and you will be able to extend your borders and discover that, ultimately, there are no frontiers at all. We tend naturally towards growth. It is just that some people, with their attitude and life style, do not allow it to show.

Our methods are part of life itself. You can meditate while you sweep the floor, do the washing, sing, dance, walk, eat or make love. Do what you love and, if that is not possible, love what you do.

Walk through the woods, in awareness of your breathing and your steps and, sooner or later, you will merge into the woods; once this has happened, you will taste life in all its intensity. The world needs specialists – in living.

The invisible hand of the *Pachamama* helps those who help their brother. Often the easy ways lead nowhere. Often the hard ways take in the master on the journey. Brother, are you coming? We want to share a dream with you, a dream that we have refused to give up dreaming.

Your way does not exist beforehand; it is revealed through direct experience whenever you settle into the cosmos and you melt into the *Pachamama*.

Renouncement entails an act of bravery. Words of love hold great power when they are born of a sincere being. Space does not separate but unites, just as the ocean's waters unite the fish.

We, the indigenous people, know that money can buy only what is not important. We are searching for the Invisible

Man, transparent, lucid, detached, capable of doing things unconditionally, of living the instant intensely, guided by the instinct; the being who, despite leaving his mark, does not expect anybody's applause or approval; who does not need to be understood or does not cling to the outcome and who loves unconditionally; who flows innocently along, who gives expecting nothing in return, who makes the inner-outer task into a thrilling adventure; who is beyond time and distance. That is why he is invisible because he is situated beyond rules and standards, because he has gone beyond his initial limitations, because he lives.

We probably feel nostalgic about our origins, but we also feel nostalgic about the future. The adventure of life makes sense when we place each act in the perspective of the star we are to become. When you are in your cosmic dimension, each act is a flower in your existential garden. There is no better offering than our harmonious vibration transformed into unconditional love. Matter is spiritualised and spirits materialise; it is all the same.

Only he who knows the *Janajpacha* is capable of giving, of being noble, of sharing, of healing. The way to *Janajpacha* is transparent. Many people do not see it because it is disguised as other things.

In the upward or downward labyrinth we can climb up or down at will. However, those who are not shamans should concentrate on climbing up. The *Tata Inti* is the sky's inhabitant. Each day, it dies and is reborn to remind us of the correct process. The *Pachamama* reveals its secrets to those who vibrate harmoniously.

The full cycle of the Moon teaches us the process of creation, growth, abundance, waning and death. The birth, the death and the rebirth that are seen in our myths and rites. The lake's shore is our reality, the other shore is the other reality.

Love is a foretaste of eternity, service is its methodology.

Being alive is a blessing but to be ignorant of how to live is a curse.

Are you in the place where you belong? Doing what you should do?

Energy is present when evolution is permanent.

Happiness is the best melody.

What is solitude? It is the interesting possibility of finding yourself and immensity.

What if children ruled the world and the rulers were sent to the gardens?

For us, spiritual work is not a way to salvation. It is a way, the best way, to approach life.

We forsake the world without forsaking it. We know that we are here to act, to do what each one has to do with the greatest will, enthusiasm, intention and love, without wasting time on clinging on to the outcome. All that matters is the fullness of the action; the outcome is of no importance.

If you think too much, your thoughts will turn into the walls of your prison. You will understand the spirituality of the Andean world when you cease to think so much and throw yourself into a daily experience, without fear or expectations.

We are men of the world and it is necessary to learn to live in it. However, we are also beings of another reality and therefore it is also necessary to become the invisible man, capable of approaching the other reality as fully as we do this one.

Let not your limitations be limited.

If you love life, you will be available for living.

Remember that each act and thought is a seed whose fruits you will have to reap one day. Each time you act unconditionally, you will feel the presence of the *Intij-Inti* within you.

As important as the big things that people do from time to time, are small, daily deeds. It is important for you to observe yourself in the daily and the ordinary so as to have a crystal-clear idea of the aspects that need working on.

Nature is our school, but not only visible nature; we are also invisible.

You open up to the cosmos from the minute you call your endless parade of thoughts to a halt.

We urgently need a method with which to boost and galvanise our existence. Andean shamanism offers you a natural way, as simple as it is effective, full of humour and love, of power and permanent growth. We are sacred because all the forces of the *Pachamama* dwell within us. Thought, intention and will are a powerful force, the beginning of Andean magic.

There, on the mountain, a fellow countryman on his way down met a climber on his way up. My countryman said: "Have you yet reached the summit of your inner mountain? Are you a climber on your inner mountain?" The climber, puzzled, stopped climbing and made as if to turn back. And the old man went on: "The way up the mountain is both hard and intensely purifying."

At the beginning, it proves harder because one carries the burden of one's problems, worries, fears and dependences. Little by little, the burden grows lighter and the way easier. The higher you climb, the more you feel yourself to be the mountain, invulnerable and serene, strong and meditative and, when you return, you are no longer the same.

What is the first lesson that I should learn to be admitted into the school of the Amautas?

And the old man said. "The first lesson consists of learning not to ask questions. When you are able to understand the eloquence

46

of silence, then you may ask again and, when you are entitled to ask, you will no longer want to do so, because you will have realised that asking is not important."

As he meditated, the Amauta was surrounded by animals, mostly snakes that were pleased to have his company. When he had finished, the Amauta said to them, as he set aside a snake that was reluctant to leave and lay twisting round his feet: "Well, the show is over. I cannot spend all day meditating." And he bade farewell to all.

We are like the snail, but we carry our home within instead of outside; in other words, we feel ourselves to be at home even when we are far away.

What does one have to do to get bored? This question was asked with great interest by a forest dweller. Is it difficult to learn?

And the old man replied: "What you eat is important, but the attitude with which you eat it is just as important."

When we eat, we eat.
What do I need to feel right?

Nothing. If you need something, you will never feel right. You must feel right for no reason.

*The "Ponce" monolith, standing on the central part of the second terrace
of the Temple of Kalasasaya, Tiwanaku, Bolivia*

CHAPTER TWO

Shamanism is not just Optimism

This is not a book; it is a summons to life. For almost half a century, a Quechuan elder wandered round all manner of different villages, on the coast and in the valleys, mountains and forests of South America, to take refuge afterwards in the silence of an inaccessible mountain for over sixty consecutive years. When I met him, he was able to travel anywhere he chose without leaving his mountain. On one of the few days I saw him, he introduced me to his best friend, the only being with whom he had conversed and shared experiences in the last fifty years: a tree with whom he would later discover the mission which I must accomplish – the ancestral assignment of my forefathers.

Since then, I have travelled over one hundred thousand kilometres on different continents, giving my testimony and adapting our teachings to Western understanding; ever since then, the elder and his mountain, the tree and my forefathers have travelled with me, dressed as invisible beings.

My tree and I have written down these reflections for you. They will enable you to discover and release the enormous potential within you. Do not be satisfied with only one reading. The deep message is revealed little by little as your awareness of these teachings becomes something more than an intellectual excursion into the realm of words.

There are things that are not true in this reality, but are evident and undeniable in the other. I live on the border between this and the other reality, in that liberated zone from which both realities can be approached. What I do is neither true nor false, nor is the intellect the right instrument with which to understand it.

When you tune into the *Pachamama*, you discover that everything is magic and the secrets of the Universe are gradually revealed to you. Come to the initiation offered to you by the *Pachamama*; it is an initiation into life, within the cosmic dimension.

What are you waiting for? Talk to the Sun and the mountain until you come to form part of them. Do you want to change? Use the powers of the *Pachamama*: they are there for you to take, in the form of trees, stones and the dawn. Tune into the *Pachamama* and you will see that you are not alone. Start walking and shed your problems onto the *Pachamama* and find support in the cosmos.

In Andean shamanism, a superior magic art, the most important step is the discovery of the supreme art of living, transformed within the relentless wayfarer as he climbs to the mountain top. In the garden of your heart, start nurturing the trees of patience, love, humour, tolerance, fraternity, sincerity, creativity. Sprinkle them daily with the water of your experiences to make them grow so that, as each day passes, you may find refuge in that wonderful inner woodland whenever you need it.

Keep the fire of your heart alight and the winter of indifference will turn into spring on your arrival. Tell the North wind of your frustrations and the East wind of your troubles. If you let him, Brother Wayra will carry your heavy load, leaving you free for the rest of the journey.

Bear in mind that the Sun rises every day, reminding you that it is never too late to start again. Remember that it does not matter how dark was the darkness which came before dawn; just realise that there will be no holding back of your own dawn light once you are ready to set forth. Live in a state of dawn.

Take a long, hard look at a river, a stream or the sea from a nearby rock, melt into it until you are turned into water and, if your mind is free of all thought, you will begin to see how your repressed inner capacities slowly rise to the surface.

Do not make techniques an end in themselves. Some people miss a meal because they are too busy admiring the cutlery. There are people who die of hunger in the middle of a banquet.

Are you alive? Life begins when you find your place in the *Pachamama*. Then, whatever you do, the result will no longer matter. Only the fullness with which you throw yourself into each act will be of significance. The result depends on a number of factors. Do not try to force events. That would be like shouting to make it rain.

You are an unfinished poem that carries on writing the verses of this experiential poem through each intention and action. Your life will be an anthology of poetry from the minute you say that it shall be so.

One day, when your steps take you away from the set routine, you will find life. One day, any day, could be that day.

Brother, do not show me your outer appearance when your worth is in your essence. Do not complain that the way to the mountain is hard. Instead, set yourself to moving forward only today, each day today, never tomorrow. If you go barefoot through the forest in the form of a travelling tree, if at dawn you clothe yourself in breezes and dance without thought or haste, the birds will join the party of your life, alongside the butterflies and the river; later on, a chorus of stars will burst into their song of lucidity.

Sunrise over Lake Titicaca

You are a gift of love, the fire that gives light and warmth.

You are an opportunity to grow, to fall, to rise and to be born again.

Take care, brother, take care of your body; it is a posy of flowers in a beautiful garden, or a vulnerable boat on which to cross to the other harbour.

No, the way is not paved beforehand. It is your steps that make the way as you go along, your intentions and actions that open you up to new dimensions. Not even the blackest darkness will stop you from seeing the light when you look with your heart. Not even the most formidable difficulties will take you from your path when you understand that your only destiny is to grow.

I feel happy because, as each day dawns, so emerges the reminder that it is possible to be born again, that it is never too late to be reborn. Silence is the stream in which your inner self is reflected; do not fill it with a cloud of words. That would only reflect your outer self.

Forget what you know and clothe yourself in humility. Those who know much prevent themselves from attaining the knowledge worth knowing. If you move relentlessly throughout the night, you will reach the dawn of your life, and there you will remain for every minute of every day.

Go and light the fire of your heart. Warmth in the form of love will rouse many from their sleepy sluggishness. A look, a gesture, an intention or a tiny action, these are the best ways to pay homage to Creation, together forming a huge stride in the right direction.

At any moment, a flower appearing in the midst of unyielding cement, performing an act of utter bravery, will serve as a reminder that, with love, all is possible.

If you are so wishing,
you are that flower
and all beings converging
in you, growing
with you.

I am full of universe,
you must feel it, beyond the verse,
I am all, one and diverse,
like you.

Always carry with you
a piece of silence,
use it as a protective poncho
when meaningless talk becomes
a frivolous, persistent humming
and tries to take you over with impunity.

Always carry with you
a splinter from a star
and wherever you are,
your presence will serve as a reminder
that life is beautiful,
that eternity opens its arms
in an intention.

Sitting in the shade
of the tree of my forefathers,
feeling that life is running through our veins
like rivers of eternity
bubbling with the desire to burst out

in the form of opportunity.
Sitting, on the edge of an intention,
waiting for you – in life.

I am the evening
of an evening at twilight.
You are the dawn
of a morning awakening.
We are parts of the same day
that daily returned.

You are not alone,
you are with you.

If your body is your temporary clothing, neither spoil nor tear it
because you are not allowed to be naked here.
  Only the ignorant find enjoyment in humiliating others; those
with knowledge find enjoyment in helping all their brothers, in
respecting the whole of Creation.
  The grey of dusk falls gently on us;
night comes upon us, clad in a dark suit,
it comes gradually;
day breaks and,
little by little, light appears;
then will come spring,
without any haste, clad in flowers.

Only man,
blinded by his own stupidity,
wants to understand it all,
to find a quick lift

so as to approach essential knowledge there
and then.
The grey of dusk falls gently on us
.and man, in his haste, falls too –
with a great clang!!!

I touch myself
and I feel the energy.
In the mirror I see me
and it is a living cosmos that I see.
We are more than what is seen,
we are capable of more than is believed,
we've been given permission to work miracles!
we are committed to working the miracle,
to discovering the supreme art of living.

Seize the mirror of the external,
it is just a brittle illusion.
what are you waiting for?
When you look at your brother,
look inside, look at the essence
and not at deceptive appearances.

It is so beautiful,
as I approach essence,
a light shines in my heart.

Welcome to life!
It is simply a question of being alive
each day,
of not allowing oneself to be bamboozled

by the blandishments of those
who try to sell you the alternative
of going through life like a
walking dead man.

If you raise yourself above your reason
and you lie back on your heart,
then you will have entered the cosmic dimension.
If you spend a minute
of every day in silence,
you are building the right setting
for the voice of the *Pachamama*
to tell you of the place it has reserved for you.

What is life?
Life, your life is an opportunity,
a summons to permanent creation.
Life flows through my life,
abounding and imaginative.
Join in with life!

You are as important for the planet as the Earth is for the Universe. You are insignificant and infinite, all and nothing at all. And, on this trip, you are in charge of yourself. The best contribution you can make to the world is to live happily. Are you making that contribution?

If you look around and, wherever you look, you find beauty and teachings, then you have discovered the meaning of life.

I was walking alone in the mountains and very much alone did I feel on that particular day. And I found a flower bearing but one leaf. It was peering from amid the rocks in all its red splendour. I caressed it and, as I did so, an unknown, tender voice said to me: "I Love You". Never again have I felt alone.

And we played with the clouds. The girl who was with me, I and the mountain, spent the morning playing with the clouds. Towards noon, we felt thirsty and it began to rain; we felt cold and the Sun came out; we danced with the Sun until it grew tired and went behind the mountain to rest. When we were making ready to go down, the stars started shining their light and at once joined the party.

When you see that reason is unable to understand, you will see that mere intellect is no use, that there are things which are untrue in this reality but are true in the other.

Shall we play with the clouds?

The party of your life will begin when you realise that not everything should be referred back to the intellect. Until you discover the liberating, transforming force of the Pachamama, you will be alone wherever you are and whoever you are with.

One night, I dreamt that the earth, tired of waiting, had a violent reaction. The ground opened up and the mountains started moving; the clouds formed an air force and the trees grew so high that they touched the sky. When I awoke, I asked myself: does contemporary man need such tough lessons to be able to learn that his mission in life is not to destroy or to vanquish his fellow man?

Day after day, I dream that it is still possible to live, hand in hand with nature.

"What am I supposed to do with my life?" a young man asked me defiantly.

The same as a plant: grow. All we have to do is grow; growing covers all. If you allow the best part of your life to be taken away from you, almost one day from each day, you will have come to the earth for nothing. If you have no time to sense your life and to sense nature, nothing important will ever happen in the course of your existence.

Come, open your window to freedom.

I have no future. I just have a wonderful, eternal present.

Winning or losing is of no matter, the main thing is to grow day by day.

Each day is an invitation to a new, creative invention.

Come and let us dream aloud and remind others of the shoreless possibility of dreaming.

What do I need to feel well? Nothing: if what you want is to live to the full and you are available for life, then you need nothing else. Being alive is reason enough to feel good. If, however, you seek more reasons, then you will have set off down the path of misery.

"I have made so many mistakes," one woman said regretfully, "that I no longer have any hope in anything."

The Sun is born, it follows its course and, as it dies, it makes way for darkness. Yet, when the absence of light is at its peak, the Sun starts to show itself again. "The *Tata Inti* is reborn day after day, reminding us of our own capacity for transformation and rebirth," said the old man as he pointed towards the East.

"Despite all my great efforts, my life is still going wrong: it's as if misfortune were my shadow," bemoaned a young man.

Living is a wonderful adventure but it is, above all, this very moment. Give yourself the freedom to make a mistake and start doing things just for the sake of doing them. Never mind the outcome, nothing is either good or bad, it all boils down to teachings from which we must learn. Once you are able to put this into practice, you will see how that so-called misfortune vanishes and that sense of uneasiness disappears.

No, brother, if you complain of your sickness, you deprive yourself of the chance to discover the message attached to all forms of distress. It is also through sickness that the *Pachamama* speaks to us, encouraging us to return to the path of health. Use your illness to redesign your way of life and you will find that, above and beyond its symptoms, your ailment is an opportunity, there for you to take.

The ancestral side of wisdom offers to the humble direct access to an inexhaustible source of knowledge, a knowledge which does not stem from intellectual effort or higher education. Approach that knowledge, it is a part of your own selves.

If we fear death, we also fear life and one cannot live with fear. He who fears will always be part of the audience. What life requires, however, is direct involvement, people who are daring enough to live to the full in an act of unceasing courage. When that fullness becomes part of your life, no fear, even less the fear of death, will overcome you. Remember that death is no more than the door to another life; that nothing, except stupidity and ignorance, can happen to you and that a new era, cleansed of all fear, will begin in your life when you say so.

Freedom lives within me with complete impunity. I sense that everything belongs to me because I am the owner of nothing and of no one. I am like the wind, flaunting its freedom in wide open spaces; freedom lives within me because on nothing do I hold a deed of ownership.

It will all begin on the day you are filled with the desire to live with no conditioning factors or fears. Allow yourself to be happy: in fact, you have no right to go through life in a state of unhappiness.

Love is the road to eternity, the silence of the method used to gain access to happiness. Come! Stop chasing down the highway of the sane and start living the dream of the crazy. All the evidence points to it: lucidity is not compatible with sanity.

God gazes down on us from his realm of light through the door of the *Janajpacha*; the *Inti*, with the day. At night, he watches us from each point of light, sculptured in the darkness. Our cells are the body's stars, the heart is the Sun, lighting the path.

And that day, the butterflies flew; it was the first day of their lives ... and the last. Instinctively, each instant was soaked up by the butterflies, showing that the present is eternal when we throw ourselves into it, that it is possible to fly high when we are willing to live.

Come! Wake up to the sacred! Let not your body be the tomb of the soul, nor your mind the prison of your spirit. To live in a prison is a question of options. To carry the weight of distress is a matter of choice. Transform yourself, grow wings and fly upwards to the pinnacle of freedom. Nobody can help you escape from your prison. Only your own wings can do that.

Nothing can be brought to you by those who have taken the option of the inner prison. A little help may be afforded you by those who have come out of their cell and who know freedom. Nonetheless, each route is unrepeatable so do not make any false moves: the way is made by you and your circumstances. The best way to accomplish things is to do them. You will discover the new only when you are ready to give up the old, that cloud which is blurring your vision. Come, take the way back to the sources; come, take the way that is paved with life.

One day, the mountain called to me. Each and every day, the mountain, the river, the tree, the forest, the star and the dawn summon you to life. There is nothing so thrilling as living to the full.

Gateway into the temple of Machu Picchu

One prophecy speaks of the revelation of Andean knowledge to the West; another says that not all is lost.

Join in with life. Love is the gateway to a full life. We know that our only task is to discover a full life. Evolution is not an end, nor is its route a straight line. Evolution is both the means and the end, the return home for those who do not stay behind to take a siesta. If you find life boring, then you have not yet discovered the adventure of inner growth.

In a decrepit world like the West, it is not enough to speak out against the system; it is necessary to take care not to reproduce it with our desires or to play its game through our actions. Come, let us fuse with the *Pachamama* and journey to the Universe within you. We are not fighting to win but to live with the fullness and intensity with which the butterfly flies across the one day of its life.

For how much longer will modern man feel afraid to lead a meaningful, complete life? It is time to step out from the cave and see the light outside. It is time to live. Each intention is a word, each action a verse in the existential poem you write in this sequence of experiences. When we feel, our limits expand towards the infinite. It is then that we feel ourselves to be a piece of the Universe, dressed like a man.

The *Intij* and the *Killa* have their route; they cannot suddenly be born one day in some other place or stop halfway. The stars have their place and their brilliance; we, as beings, all have our route and our place. Whenever you fail to be in the place marked out for you, you will find problems instead of opportunities, stumbling blocks instead of challenges. Nevertheless, everything is designed to spur your progress.

If each of your actions bears the hue of reverence, it will also carry the warmth of life and the strength of harmony. If you act in accordance with what you think and, as you wait, your expression is one of patience, then you have understood the transcendental sense of your life, above and beyond living for the sake of work, amusement and eating. Each moment is a well of eternity; it is neither long nor short, it is just an opportunity.

When we throw ourselves into life, we find out that it is something more than its outward description. Without any hesitation, we acknowledge that we do not fear error. Life is an opportunity to live spontaneously, decisively, with courage and will. Life is an appointment with the impossible; a sublime crossroads where miracle and fullness meet. possibility and opportunity

True progress is spiritual; real wealth is to be found within; true beauty lies in the soul; a full man is as great as the Universe, he is the Universe itself, dressed like a man.

We are summoning you to an act of bravery for only the brave know how to love; the act of loving is the sacred way to the *Janajpacha*, transformed into the invulnerable wayfarer. The wayfarer we are inviting you to become moves on with an inner light, with the lucidity bestowed upon him by the link with the *Intij-Inti*.

The heart of the wayfarer is the *Pachamama* itself and, as such, is an endless source of love. Inspired by the travelling *T'unupa*, the wayfarer has cut through fear to move ahead relentlessly, living each instant with intensity, plunging into each experience.

It is important to remember the need to find the way, to be willing to shake off the chains that hold you to things and even to people. To move forward, you must be ready to go on giving things up, because it is only through saying goodbye to the secondary that you will be able to gain access to the essential.

Walking down the path is not a way of life, it is life itself. The alternative is the path of non-life, of insignificant existence. To walk is to progress, to progress is to grow, to grow is to love, to love is to live.

Turn yourself into the wayfarer on the way up to the conquest of your inner mountain. Handle lovingly the piece of the *Pachamama* which is you. If fear feeds off ignorance, find refuge and drink at the fountain of wisdom, the supreme cleanser of all fear.

We are humbly pouring out a rain of experiences to reach the innermost depths of your hearts and water the seed of simplicity, of spontaneous innocence and sweetness, of humanity, so sadly lacking at times such as these, times of unpunished, advocated inhumanity. Travel to your inner self and you will discover your outer mission.

At a time when modern man devotes his days to hoarding more and more instead of to self-improvement, Andean shamanism is a summons to a full life, beyond the empty word and the heavy head.

The pity of it all is that city dwellers do not know what they really need and, in their confusion, run hither and thither in an attempt to satisfy unnecessary needs born of their burden of anguish and their sickness.

The *Pachamama* showed me the way of simplicity, the path of humility, the meaning of tolerance and the sacred, the importance of creativity, the power of love and humour; the *Pachamama* showed me the sure way of life. Tune into the *Pachamama*. Be calm: the very fact of discovering genuine life will endow you with great strength to enable you to continue on your way.

Happiness is revolutionary,
plenitude is subversive,
come to life and its poetic dimension,

join in the cosmic dance,
this sequence of sublime unexpected events,
this whirlpool of experiences,
a spiral of occurrences.

Come and drink from the fountain of the creative imagination, the mainstay of the *Pachamama* in its multiple dimension.

You can become a stockbroker, dealing in changes in your life.

Every now and again, we ask ourselves what we are doing with that wonderful opportunity called 'life' – and always the answer is a different attitude. The doors of the *Pachamama* are permanently closed to those who remain slaves to their reason and their minds.

The only indispensable act of loyalty consists of being faithful to life, by showing a readiness to live every minute of every day. There is neither time nor space when your consciousness and each step you take beat in time with the *Janajpacha*. Plunge into the *Pachamama* and, in every single situation, depth will return to your vision and unity to your life.

Andean shamanism is an invitation to take part in creation with the best of wills, in the context of the cosmic dimension. The trouble is, people do not know how to live and, until the supreme art of living is discovered, there is nothing but artificial happiness, intermingled with depression and stress.

When I meditate, I go back into silence, taking my place beyond distance. There are people who waste their lives trying to gain time. There are people who spend their lives not living. Little does it matter what you do if your inner attitude is not consistent with your actions.

The fear of death conceals the fear to live fully. Death will accompany you to remind you that, today, it is life's turn. The purest silence will give you back your freedom.

Problems? What problems? If you think you have problems, then you have not yet settled into the cosmos!

To pursue the satisfaction of your desires is to take a non-stop flight to the nearest gaol. Brother, you who wish to share your truth, clean up your inner halls before stepping out into the world. Only when your windowpanes are polished will the inner light be able to shine forth. Make this life into a heaven or a hell: it is up to you. Both stand before you, within your reach.

Assign a piece of silence to each day: this is the best existential dessert at a banquet of the spirit, destined to turn into everlasting wellbeing.

When I fail to understand, I consult the trees or the rivers. They tell me that it is not important to have a clear idea about everything, that it is not possible to know the way before going down it.

If you begin the day in silence, contemplating the dawn;
if you go through the day, dancing at dusk;
and you receive the night, playing with the stars;
and when you lay down your head in the darkness,
peace keeps you company in your solitude;
then you have discovered the transcendental quality of life.

Life is a sacred space which we must inhabit without disrespect or fear; it is a path to be trodden with respect and decisiveness. Are you sure of being alive at times like this when there are so many dead beings trudging the streets?

Some people, oblivious to the opportunity of being the condor and of the great chance to fly, choose to slither down the blind alleys of trifling normality. Do not worry: all you can do for other people is live well. Your permanent wellbeing, your unfailing inner peace, will make an adequate contribution of your presence, even when silent.

If you still have not tuned into the *Pachamama*, life remains unknown to you. He who has not found the magical sense of life cannot but be distressed and sick. A bird cannot fly before it comes out of its shell; one cannot discover the light outside without leaving the cave. Meaningful life is hidden behind apparent life. The fear of death vanishes when you stop clinging on and your dedication to life grows.

The *luluwen* attacks those who do not remain on the alert. It is these people too who will be converted by the forces of materialism and robotisation into walking dead men, bereft of imagination, beings in their basest form. Man is but a finite, fleeting statement of infinity and eternity.

Stretch your heart to the cosmic dimension,
and you will see how all your intention
converges into living with devotion.

Gaining access to life entails tuning the strings of your heart beforehand
and feeling the throbs of the *Pachamama*.

Without freedom there is no inner growth,
without inner growth there is no real freedom.

Come and let's soak up life,
abundance, it's not a lost cause yet;
come, stop wasting energy,
it is still possible to live every instant of every day.
Beyond your mistakes you are there too,
waiting for another chance.

Altiplano and Andes, Bolivia

The complaint is a declaration of fecklessness made by someone who conceals a pitiful vacuum behind each experience. If you have not planted flowers on the inside, you will see only thorns on the outside.

Be as the *Pachamama*, infinite as the Universe, humble as the flower.

There are people who possess many things and yet they do not possess themselves. How absurd the human being is when he does not begin at the beginning. What modern man cannot understand with his mind, he calls death; it is just a different life.

Brother,
if there is something to be feared,
let it be the failure to use life to grow;
the only way to receive death well
is to learn to live to the full.

What is life?
Life is a challenge.
Who am I?
You are the wayfarer, the feet that the way
is longing to feel upon it.
A way without a wayfarer is no way at all,
just as a wayfarer at a standstill serves no purpose.
But, what if I cannot rise to the challenge of moving on
and am unable to overcome the hurdles in
my way?

Winning or losing is of no matter; the point is to live to the full. Throw yourself fully and openly into everything you do, big or small, and forget about the outcome.

The best way to make a mess of something is to make obsessive attempts at doing it right. It is important not to be preoccupied by the outcome, as this has a paralysing effect which prevents you from enjoying the journey. The goal is not at the end of your path; it is spread out into each step. If you understand this, then you are inoculated against frustration and the inaugural ceremony of your life has taken place.

Is it important to be efficient in life?
Apart from living, nothing is important.
Be full and everything will run smoothly.
How can I overcome my fears?
Accept death, your death, and free yourself
of the unnecessary desire for the approval of
others;
give yourself the freedom to make a mistake,
find enjoyment in all you do, especially in your mistakes;
be a successful failure – behind each failure lies a lesson for you to
learn;
in other words, failure does not exist;
you will begin a fearless life when you say so!

By our example, we teach that what is lacking here is the courage to love. All everybody needs is love. Why is love so important? Because, if you love, you see the essence as opposed to the appearance, and everything becomes transparent and bright.

No, brother, don't be sad;
don't you realise that your limitations
are really your own potential
awaiting release?

A villager returning to her home on the Bolivian altiplano

If you tune into the *Pachamama*,
you will find that a star
guides you constantly along your way,
it's never lonely, the way –
so that each time you make up your mind
to take another step, you have
the entire Universe on your side.

Is it necessary to think?
To think is to produce birds –
but let them fly,
because if they make nests in your head,
they will, one day, become unbearable.

Silence is the key to the door of your mind.
Three men were arguing, contending
for the ownership of truth.
How dare you contend
for the truth like that when the truth
may be attained only through experience
and understood with silence?
What is the flower?
The flower is the smile of the *Pachamama*.
When you discover life, what a surprise!
The whole of life is contained in a smile.
Life is a cosmic prank.

Our proposal is this:
to move off the highways
of a present paved with lies
onto paths of soil, grass and flowers,
where life goes on twenty-four hours a day.

What is life?
Life is a voyage
over the sea of circumstance,
on the vulnerable ship
which is our body.
He who fails to take care of his vessel
ends up shipwrecked
and misses the excitement of the trip.

The stars have a language only the humble
understand.

Life is at once the way and the wayfarer, that ongoing traveller,
sound and serene in step.
You are a wayfarer.

Some people live as if nothing was happening and, in fact,
nothing is happening in the routine of their existence.
We are weaving, as of old,
weaving a different future,
a life in which the human is present
and abundance no more absent.
We are spreading, above all, a teaching
to be understood through experience.
Would you like to join the guild
of the existential weavers
of the New Humanity?

Brother, each one is responsible for this opportunity,
received from the immense potential bestowed upon him
– Live!

If it is impossible to go on surviving like this, what are you
waiting for?
The moment we've been waiting for has arrived and in turn, is
waiting at your side.

Ignorance has still not been abolished
and destructive inhumanity lives on with impunity
in many Western people.
Still has fear not been uprooted from life; there is poison instead
of food.
Still are people dying without having found out what they had
this present for.
Still...

And from comfortable prisons,
amid puffs of smoke and other addictions,
modern man speaks – of freedom.
If the world is hopelessly decrepit,
what are you waiting for?
Allow your steps to take another direction.

Fear?
Why?
At worst, we shall die,
but, as we are eternal,
we shall have another chance
and again we shall return.
Fear?
It isn't worth being afraid;
real life begins where fears end.

The Sun-Man, or the "Weeping God", the central figure of The Gate of the Sun, Tiwanaku, Bolivia

CHAPTER THREE

And the Elders Told...

"Old man, I am cold." "Son," the old man said, "the mountain is warm and the rain a caress, when you carry within you the *Intij Inti* and you see yourself as part of the *Pachamama*. Whenever you feel cold, merge into the mountain; when in darkness, melt into the Sun; when you want to move on, blend into the wind and, when you want to approach the *Chej Pacha*, change into the now flowing, now evanescent water, rising invisibly to the *Janajpacha*.

"You're cold? No, my son, you have life and a wonderful opportunity to use it with respect and imagination. Don't use your complaints as a constant excuse to avoid life!"

They said to him, "I want to know nature." "You are nature," he replied. "All you have to do is stop thinking and start observing, see from the depths of your vision, feel intensely, feel everything, both inside and out. Little by little, you'll discover that frontiers come falling down and you become what you want to know. That is true knowledge, the way which will lead you back to your real dimension."

The birds and the trees, the butterflies and the flowers have all gone. Where are the crystalline springs? What has become of the endless symphony that charmed our days? For how much longer will modern man go on killing in the name of life? For how much longer will the silent accomplices stand by and watch the slaughter of Mother Earth with indifference? How much longer?

Suffering is reserved for those who violate the laws of nature. Love is the fundamental law of the *Pachamama*. There is no time, there are several times. Each thing, each living being has its own time.

"We are immortal, we are eternal like the invisible trees," said the grandfather's grandfather as he was led to the stake, accused of being a witch doctor.

We, the people of the Andes, know that life ends nowhere; it just wears different clothes when it leaves this present behind.

We are farmers. Day by day, we cultivate our lives, sprinkling them with the water of knowledge, the inexhaustible spring of wisdom, and we offer them warmth from the rays of the Sun fused into love.

Brother, the Earth is the visible presence of the invisible *Intij Inti*. Man is the cosmic space, enjoying the wisdom of the *Pachamama*. We are retrieving the paths trodden by our forebears, the same paths that our children and grandchildren will tread when the past, dressed as the future, becomes the present again on this cyclical parade of ages and times that come and go relentlessly.

He who harms his own self shows a lack of respect for his brothers and offends the *Pachamama*. Freedom ends when someone starts to harm his body or his environment.

A travelling fellow countryman who had chosen to go on long therapeutic journeys into faraway places used to say: "No, I am not alone. The *Tata Inti* embraces me by day and the stars guide my steps by night. "I am not alone, the *Pachamama* travels with me."

Our forefathers visit us in our dreams, they talk to us and we dance together. Our forefathers know that now is the time to go out into the world, to reach all places in the form of music, dances or silent experiential knowledge.

"We are not going to die," said the village elders, "until amends have been made to the *Pachamama*, until the trees are respected again and the animals treated like brothers. "We are not going to die without giving a living testimony that life is sacred and different."

One of the forest dwellers used to tell this tale:

"My brother committed suicide on the day he discovered that the place where he had been brought up, a majestic wood, had been bought and made into a ranch to fatten cattle whose meat would feed the faces of those wealthy, obese people from the North, who find it hard to lose weight even if they go on a diet. Grandfather died of sorrow while he embraced his friend, the tree. An electric saw had put an end to that eighty-year friendship."

And, in disbelief and sorrow, the forest dweller listened to the detailed account of a bloody destruction. "The massacre of our forefathers", he thought, "is celebrated by the same people who came here five hundred years ago and are back again, in the form of their descendants."

And the llama shepherd sang as he caressed the silence, carving exquisite figures at each pause, without haste, without time, with the sound in the background of Brother Wayra, who occasionally joined the recital. The shepherd sang songs impossible to repeat. "The mountains teach me," he used to say. "I sing as I travel to the home of my ancestors; I sing as I play with my grandchildren as yet unborn."

They took down our temples and used them as quarries. Today, all that remains are a few traces. However, the most important temples are in our hearts and thence we shall start to go forth from now on, with the knowledge that they were unable to destroy a teaching whose purpose is to rebuild the state of consciousness in which destiny has thought it right that we should live.

Children know how to be happy; llamas, cows and alpacas are exemplary models of serenity; ants, of the relentless march forward, and the condor of the transcendental flight.

We, the indigenous people, have not forgotten that life is the best teacher when our hearts are open. We do not measure life in terms of years, nor do we value people on the basis of their qualifications and titles. We do not acknowledge frontiers, nor do we believe in those who do not practise what they preach. We, the indigenous people, are the savages of the world because we have not renounced innocence nor have we sacrificed spontaneity, because we continue to go through the world dressed in silence and humility, empty of arrogance and full of love for Creation in its entirety.

We are simple men; we feel that simplicity is the way to the light, the sacred Sun of Suns.

No, brother, our handicrafts are not beautiful just because they are brightly coloured and meticulously carved. They are beautiful because they bear prophecies and millenary teachings; every single detail is a symbol, and every symbol the substance of our perception.

"They have always lied to us," bemoaned an old man on the mountain. "The only difference is that they have updated their hypocrisy and some lie to us scientifically while others lie to us sincerely."

A fellow countryman ran through the streets of a city at top speed, much to the surprise of the robotised pedestrians and the stress-ridden drivers. After a long chase, the countryman was arrested by the police. "What crime have you committed? Whom have you robbed?" the policeman asked accusingly. The countryman answered, "I am escaping from the hell into which I was about to fall." And on he ran, towards the outskirts of that huge city.

We are wandering stars on the way to eternity, in love with lucidity, seduced by abundance. We are shooting stars, rebuilding our eternity.

Modern man lives in a system through which he is made to suffer from selective amnesia. He is forgetful of the most important, the immense power he carries inside, but he is obsessively, distressingly mindful of his mistakes and of matters of no importance.

Some people expect to see the invisible, but fail to realise that it does not appear in visible clothing and cannot be so recognised. We, the Andean people, know that, behind the visible and the fleeting, lie the invisible and the eternal. That is why we are not concerned about time and appearances.

"Why don't city folk touch one another?", a forest child asked his mother. "Why do they hide their bodies under coloured leaves? Why do they walk so fast? Why don't they sleep by night and dance by day? Why do they all look so serious? Why don't they embrace the trees and taste their fruits? Why do they prefer to devour tins and strange fruits that are born of no tree?"

A forest dweller used to say that the best time to go harvesting is at night. Our fathers learned from the fathers of their fathers and taught their children. They taught us to see with our entire bodies and to read the invisible messages written in nature. If you want to see far into the distance, you must close your eyes.

"Something strange is happening to the white man," remarked a group of mountain dwellers anxiously one night as they sat in a circle round a flickering fire, motionlessly contemplating their many-coloured ponchos. "Something strange is happening to the white man," repeated the oldest. "It's as if he were ill and there were no cure for his sickness. He knows this and, in his hopelessness and despair, it's as if he's made up his mind to destroy as much as he can, including his own self and his children."

"He seems to have gone mad," said another, "so utterly, uncontrollably mad that he does increasingly stupid things. The fact of the

City Centre, Buenos Aires, Argentina

matter is that he is going from bad to worse and does not seem to be aware of it."

"Perhaps he's drunk," added another, "from everything he has produced and invented."

"Then again, perhaps he's half-asleep," suggested yet another, "and he thinks that everything is a nightmare from which he cannot awake."

"But he must wake up," said another firmly. "Things cannot go on like this."

"Brothers," said the oldest, "he is not likely to wake up until he realises that he is asleep. All we can do is be ourselves so that he may see in us the proof that life is different and that, despite all, it is still time to live."

In my heart, I feel that more and more white people are returning to the arms of the *Pachamama*.

Come and let us share a new dawn, lying back in the cosmos, vibrating as one body with the diverse Universe.

Come and let us meet, above and beyond words, in the invisible garden where only the humble may come.

The *Pachamama* looks after you – especially when you look after it.

Brother! Wait a minute! Where are you running, blindfolded so? Why are you walking on the edge of an abyss? Brother, we, the indigenous people, have been walking barefoot through life for thousands of years, and we have learned that there is no goal other than life in the form of a path, the path of learning. The goal is present in each trip.

Come and let us speak in silence. There are no words left.

If you allow comfort to make you sluggish, then you will prevent your flower from blooming.

We do not cut the wings of the butterfly that is us.

While modern man is forever asking himself questions, we are simply contemplating.

It is a matter of choice whether you make life difficult or not.

We speak in silence and travel without leaving our mountain. We know that, in this time, we have to say something; we are sure that the best way to do so is in the constellation made up by: silence, a look, a presence, music, dance and, sometimes, an absence.

We know that our message will not fit into a bottle made of words. My forebears and I invite you to a reunion, beyond the realm of words, in life at its full. Are you coming?

I take care of my canoe and my body so as to be able to reach the other shore, the other harbour. I have come down from the Andes to the threshold of your hearts, like the postman bringing an urgent message, a past experience with which to live the present, an existence in which life is not absent.

Come and let us play with the stars,
sleeping glow-worms glimmering in their lucidity.
Come, let us fly like butterflies.
Step out of routine, forget all that,
forget anything that, in the name of life,
is killing you night after night, day after day.

Come to the forest of your heart
and climb up your inner mountain;
life starts when you stop thinking.
Come! It is only a matter of living.

Have you still not talked to the trees or listened to the mountains? Have you still not made a pact with our brothers, the animals? Have you still not learned the language of the clouds? I am sorry, but to go through life like a transcendental deaf-mute is not pleasant. Come and reconcile yourself to the Pachamama.

It was raining one day – in my heart. The Tata Inti descended the stairway to the *Janajpacha*, the rainbow; I struggled my way up it and, when I arrived at the top, I found, swathed in transparent light, people of the most diverse origins. They all belonged to the universal religion, to the unmistakable, everlasting truth, the passport to eternity.

It was raining one day, and the unknown person I could see coming along the path in a blaze of light may have been you.

Although I did not know you, I could sense, yes, I could sense that your heart was beating; that it was not by chance that this message had been placed in your hands.

As you know, we are and always have been brothers, making the return journey home. There shall we meet, if you move without haste or halt.

The mountains taught us that, when you are divided by words, you should look to unifying silence for help.

Western brother, do not judge us for being different. When you lower your accusing finger, you will discover that appearance vanishes to make way for the unifying essence.

Western brother, may our example be for you an experiential argument, a point of reference for a full, transcendental life on your voyage of discovery to this wonderful opportunity: immensity transformed into an experiential sequence.

'Each day, on awaking, the elder would say: *Pachamama*, give me the clarity with which to see the essence instead of the appearance; let my breathing merge into yours and, like a breeze, blow itself clearly along. *Pachamama*, give me strength to go on, let nothing take me from my path. I want to return my essence to its origin and be, once more, a star in the firmament.

I am complete, the entire Universe in a nutshell dwells within me.

Our forebears did not die, they settled anew in the cosmos; and they are with us today in the form of a cloud, a mountain, a star or a sunset.

Our forebears travel before us, leaving their footprints of humility and life.

We are petals from the same flower, we are enveloped by the same perfume, we are nourished from the same root. There is no greater rival than our own stupidity.

The Wayra spoke to our forefathers, saying, in a clear voice: "Brothers, you can fly like me, relentless, invulnerable; you can fly from the minute you change into an open space, like me."

I have wandered through your cities and my eyes have been at pains to take in those strange, inexplicable sights: people rushing about, people lying, even to themselves, people wearing shackles and chains, people killing, people destroying the *Pachamama*. And my steps turned back to the inner paths whence I have returned with the message of my ancestors.

All the words in the world
fit into a splinter of silence,
into the innocent eyes of the forest dweller,
into the majestic flight of the condor over the Andes.
Reconcile yourself to silence,
the voiceless voice of the *Pachamama*.

Late afternoon sunlight lighting up the terraces of Machu Picchu

Western brother,
we want to tell you a secret,
we are all brothers,
we are all trees in the same wood,
we all drink from the same fountain,
we all share the same cosmic breath,
life is a community of hearts.

Come, let us tell it with the wind,
that we are all brothers,
that there is no need to make things so complicated.
Come, let us dance in the rain,
let us reconcile ourselves to innocence
so that we may feel that
we are all travelling companions,
that a common destiny awaits us,
that we must go beyond that which keeps us apart.

Climb the mountain,
learn of its stillness;
go down the river,
learn of its transparence;
raise your eyes to the star,
imitate its lucidity;
feel the *Huayra*,
acquire its invulnerability.

Climb to life from the depths
where, in the name of life,
people become sick and kill.
Climb! In the life that is real,
no lasting distress will you feel.

Modern brother, my elder brothers have bidden me tell you that there is something wonderful that you can do for yourself. This is it, you, for yourself: live, live to the full.

Brothers, we the indigenous know that, within each person, there is light. Why do you go through life like an opaque body when you, too, have light? Why don't you share it with your brothers? Didn't your parents tell you that we are the stars of the earth?

Do not harm anybody; everybody is *Pachamama*, It is just that some have forgotten their roots. Do not allow the amnesiacs to force you to act like a fool.

Western brother, come and let us enjoy a silent conversation; or, let us turn into the condor and fly! Brother, if you come home, we can share the stars, the clouds and the wind; we can discover that all is well when it is the outcome of Love.

"The white man," said one of my countrymen, "dresses in words to hide his base bareness, his regrettable existential vacuum, filled with frivolity. The white man keeps words in his mind, in his wardrobe, in his nights and his refrigerators and in his beds and his nightmares. When white men meet, they exchange words, hollow words in an inane burbling, and so banish the silence that never lies."

He was taken prisoner for refusing to die. He was put into a mental hospital for daring to live. In the world of the sleeping, it is bad manners to stay awake. The recommended, widespread practice is to sleep with neither intention nor interruption because to wake up would disturb the sleep of the rest.

And, as the grandmother was returning home, a doctor who knew of her healing abilities approached her and asked her where she had studied.

"Son," said the grandmother, "you don't have to have academic qualifications to pick up a wounded bird from the path, you just have to know how to love. If, through studying hard, you forget how to love, then no matter how much you know, you will be of no use to anyone."

Perhaps man was not born to live at the frontier of life, to remain standing on the shore of ignorance or to roll basely through the shadows of madness. Perhaps we came to live on the banks of abundance; perhaps we came to shell the seeds of essential wisdom; perhaps somebody is fanning the flames of confusion to make us miss this wonderful opportunity.

"No longer shall I sow the land," said the old man. "I shall go to the big city and I shall scatter seed in squares and parks, on pavements and in schools, to remind people that they have forgotten about nature. I shall go to the city to sow the message of the *Pachamama* in the minds of those who have not become machines."

Early one morning, the old man opened his eyes no more. He had summoned his children to tell them to lay him down for the last time.

"The earth is calling me and the stones advise me to depart; I just want to remind you that I shall remain with you in the form of a tree.

"I can see the colourful night and the largest and shiniest of stars, I sense that my limits are disappearing ... I can see myself ... down below ... I feel sleepy ... tree, tree, tree. And from placid sleepfulness, I pass into eternity."

That morning, a tiny shoot revealed the birth of a plant. Years later, a towering tree seemed never to tire of looking into the house from beyond.

The children who had talked to the tree died, the Westernised grandchildren sold the house. One day, a tree was chopped down by the new owners. One wail after another, one for each stroke of the axe, sent shivers up and down the woodcutter's spine. He stopped working and stepped back to look at the tree. It was then that a voice could be heard, as if it came from the innermost depths of the earth, or from the immense sky or from the trunk of the tree: "We, the trees, also feel, we are willing to help man when he acts with respect, wisdom and love for the *Pachamama* and Creation. But man has forgotten to talk to us, forgotten that we are indispensable and, ignorant of the fact that we are here to help him, goes on destroying us until entire species disappear.

"My brother trees have asked me to request you to pass this message on before it's too late."

Ever since then, a man has been going from village to village, talking to the trees, wrapping them in his arms and asking them to dance.

And that night, at the same time, the ritual began; the same silence, broken only by occasional remarks from the old man, as he spoke to the *Pachamama*.

It was a ceremony to make amends to the planet, an act of love towards the Universe, a sequence of respect which would have to be followed in every home, every school, every neighbourhood so as to produce a consciousness linked to the immensity of Creation.

It is just a matter of sitting round in a circle, lighting a fire in the middle, laying out a blanket showing the three kingdoms and talking to the earth, in silence, with music or with songs.

"He died in the river," a fellow countryman said. "My brother always bathed in the river. He had been away for many a year and when he returned, he flung himself excitedly into the river never to appear again. My brother did not know that, three years before, our brother the river had died and, with it, thousands of birds and animals, thousands, ever since the factory built upstream had started operating and provided jobs for twenty.

"Twenty are paid a salary and the rest of us are paid with poison."

Child of migrant slash and burn cultivators: Maraba, Amazon basin, Brazil

In the forest, a boy asked his elder brother: "Why do city folk walk fast and hide their feet?"

And the elder brother answered: "Because they are in such a hurry that they're too embarrassed to show their feet."

"And why do they hide their bodies under coloured skins?" the boy went on.

"Because they are angry with Father Sun, they are sons with no respect for the heat of the Sun and that's why they're as pale as pale can be."

"And why do the fruits they eat have such a hard shell?"

"In truth, my brother, I think that everything is hard in the city. Our grandfather has told me that they have tall trees of stone, where they live like birds. Grandfather says that, over in the city, they neither sing at dawn nor dance at dusk. He says that they have forgotten to talk to the trees and that they don't listen to the river.

"He says that their canoes sail along the ground and that they become wicked when they sit in them."

"And why do they live in trees of stone? Stone is cold and hard," the boy insisted. "Grandfather says that they live like that because they are being punished, because they have forgotten to talk to the trees and listen to the river."

"Brother," said the boy as he stood up, "today, I haven't talked to the tree. Shall we go? I don't want to be punished and sent to live in the trees of stone."

The old man was saying farewell to his community on the high mountain which he had never left.

"Where are you going, grandfather?" they asked.

"I'm going to the city to tell the people that the earth is weeping." And the old man set off.

Many moons later, he returned and, ask him as they might, never a word did he say about what he had seen. On the mountain top, an aymara was playing his quena.

"The sky is red," he said as he paused, "because the *Pachamama* has been wounded." And he went on playing. A musical wailing, at times more like a scream, tore through the silence.

Although the old *aymara* had been dead for several years, a quena could be heard on the mountain, someone was wailing and the sky once more turned red.

One day, we, the indigenous people, were silent; now, it is our turn to speak.

One day, the people of the West spoke; now it is their turn to be silent.

Without a prolonged silence, whatever you want to say, leave it for another day.

Modern man suffers from the sickness of indifference.

A chronic illness that stops him from loving.

Modern man wants to love without giving, or is ready to give without loving.

Modern man has modernised love to such a degree that it no longer serves the purpose of loving. He loves without love and he suffers on account of it because it is so insipid.

Those who destroy the earth carry out orders issued by those who have received no order to destroy the earth.

Do not worry, brother! Things cannot go on like this. Concentrate on directing your steps in the perspective of light and life.

On the outskirts of the city, the old man was asked: "What are you thinking when you say nothing?"

"Nothing," the old man replied. "If I spent all my time thinking like the white man, I'd be living in the city."

We are sons of the Sun. The Sun lives within ourselves, producing a strong *lantin*, a basic requirement to be able to heal.

Everyone has an inner Sun from the instant they treat the Universe with love. We are all sons of the Sun, even those who live with their backs turned to it. We have been watching nature for thousands of years, listening to its advice, talking to it. What we're telling you, Western brother, is what we learn from nature. It is not a knowledge of our own, we are just passing it on.

A new world is being made ready for those who walk the earth in humility; we have seen it in dreams; our forefathers saw it too. It is a world with two Suns, where all may talk with one and all without breaking the silence.

We have come down from our mountains to return to man his ancestral memory. It is time to go back home. It is time to live, to relive the sacred teachings, rekindling the inner fire. Brother, we are here, to reconcile ourselves to the *Pachamama*.

It is time to fast and dance, to climb the sacred mountain and to journey to our own, inner mountain; it is time to cross the river to the other side.

Come, step into the canoe of knowledge and leave the shores of ignorance behind.

We live to evolve. What else could we do, if we are on our way to wonderful eternity?

We are asked who the indigenous people are that speak like this and we, in silence, tell them that we are the same who one day will die, and today, in a fraternal gesture, come with a message addressed to your heart and your yearning to return to the cosmic dimension.

No, we do not want a diploma in walking death, nor do we want to specialise in committing acts of stupidity. We shall not come out from behind the frontier of life, nor shall we reduce our existence to working for clothes, food and a house.

Market trader, Cuzco, Peru

Brother, we, through our craftsmanship, are now building the future of the native people. Come! Join in with this task, living to the full. It is all too easy to miss opportunities and to forget that, here, it is just a matter of living.

And we come together, fluidly, our hearts converging lovingly.

Come! Let us pass on our voices, experiences and breath so that, invisibly, our brother wind may carry them the length and breadth of the world, reminding us that we are all bound in the same direction.

What if this were the appointed hour? What if you found yourself in the chosen time? In silence, something new is being made ready. Let the old fade away and the new gently settle in without haste, without fear; with merriment and song, rejoicing that your pulse and that of the Universe are lovingly beginning to beat as one.

Something is happening!
Something immense is astir!
Are you still sleeping the sleep of illusion?
Are you still buying and buying and obsessively hoarding?
Something new is occurring in the lives of many,
in beings who are dressing in light
as they give and feel.
If life were infinite, I would give you an eternal kiss.
If life were an instant, I would dress in a flash of lightning
and I might even go to your heart to remind you
that this is the moment to forge ahead in evolution;
to tell you not to make matters so complicated or face life with
suffering and tears;
to remind you that we are with you, that you are not alone, that
in our indigenous
people and the whole, wide universe, you have a friend.

The next message may be different, it may be aimed at all those people who still lie to themselves. The next message will be heavily loaded for those who still live amid destruction and death. The next message won't be for you, or will it?

"People used to wonder," recalled an old man, "whether Indians are human beings. Now it is our turn to wonder whether the modern white man is, or is not, a human being."

We go along, full of love. There is no room inside us for hatred or rancour. We move forward, overflowing with innocence and spontaneity, tenderness and humility, loyal to life, hand in hand with the *Pachamama*, showing modern man our way of life.

Gone is the era of complicated answers embedded in pedantic wording that used to cloud the atmosphere at every utterance.

Simplicity is the way and humility, the method through which to understand the deepest knowledge. When this is not enough, it is time for silence.

Life is a wonderful opportunity from the moment we walk its path carrying the *Pachamama* within.

After a long absence, an indigenous woman returned to the forest where her people lived, only to find nobody there.

"Where are my sons?" she asked as she walked. "Where are my grandchildren who used to play with the insects? Where are the women who danced at dawn? Where are the robust youths who passed the toughest initiatory tests?

"Where are the fragrant flowers that played with the colourful butterflies?

"Where are the birds that sang the most beautiful songs by day to be relieved at night by a whole range of insects in chorus with the stars?

"Where are the gigantic ancient trees and their advice? Where are they all? Why have they gone? Why have they been taken away? Where are they? Where?" And she remained there weeping, clinging to a huge, felled tree.

We do not make music, we just copy the sounds of the *Pachamama*.

Which day do we devote to God? Every day.
How many hours a day? All the hours.
Once you have found the meditative dimension in all,
it matters not what you do
for you will always be with God.

Western brother, this is the voice with no interludes and no false interpretations, the voice of those who have always been silent.

As an old man said, looking down from his mountain top, not far from the city: "Modern man is a spoilt child knocking apart the house which he was given to live in."

When our forebears came to the Earth, they knew that they were carrying all that was needed to live well and to grow. We must now act and make preparations in the same way as our forebears.

When the *Intij Inti* sent us, he advised us to look after the wonderful home provided for us and, ever since then, we have been the guardians of the earth. Our silent presence is the everlasting reminder that we must love the *Pachamama*.

Our morning dance is a greeting to all of Creation, gratitude for the teaching, the joy of life.

The land in which we live is sacred and our brothers are the animals and the trees. The mountains are sacred, like the wind and the stars. We are sacred. To be unhappy and lead a life of misery is to show a lack of respect for the *Intij Inti* and to pour scorn on the sacred teachings.

Modern man has crushed the spiritualness of the world's peoples. The indigenous, as inheritors of an ancient tradition, will bring that spiritualness back, before mystic impotence and spiritual anorexia make man into a robot and the *Pachamama* into a radioactive desert.

Join life.

It is in no way uncommon for modern society's remedies to be worse than the ailment they are intended to cure. With each new remedy, the West gets worse; the more they progress, the worse they live. Western man will have to choose between progress and life.

You, Western brothers, also have an ancient tradition; you have also received a magic, ancestral inheritance: your forefathers were just like us, they knew how to talk to the trees and dance with the stars, they walked the earth respectfully and were grateful for so much wisdom written in every drop of dew, each stream of sunlight, each flight of a bird, each sunset.

Just like us, your forefathers knew that eternity flows through our veins, that it is better to wear the clothes of humility.

Perhaps it is time, Western brother, to look back at your distant ancestors: you may be quite surprised to discover that, in essence, we all speak the same language. Listen to the voice of your ancestors and follow in their footsteps.

Now that they have massacred us and pillaged our villages, to us, it seems most strange that they should propose to celebrate the genocide by dancing upon our dead.

Yes, to us, it does seem strange that they should have continued to lie to us for five hundred years. In truth, what we find less and less strange is the cynicism and the stupidity, especially when there are people who have made this into their only existential option.

Our journey to the West has an integrating purpose; it is an attempt to build a bridge between your heart and our ancestral intention.

We are a crack in the structure of society, which has always treated us with arrogance and vanity. We wear the magic tunic of the *Pachamama*, sure that this chance is unrepeatable and unique.

Survi Amerindian children watch a logging road being cut through their reservation

Photo: Mark Edwards/Still Pictures

Western brother, words are not always necessary when we embrace spontaneity and join the immenseness as one. Brother, when words do not serve and often, only tire instead, then it is time for silence.

We have journeyed long on the edge of history and when a *Pachacuti* has started to change, we have gathered all our hearts together and, between us all, we have lent wings to hope and begun to step forth, without any formulas, just to give you an embrace, that indispensable gesture; for fraternity, we are always ready.

Sitting in the shade of a memory,
on the edge of a word,
caressing the naked body of unbroken silence.

Sitting, in my liberated zone,
where no word is necessary,
on the edge of my circumstance,
next to its absent presence.

Sitting, writing out for you
a message that lies above and beyond words,
in that sacred place where we shall meet,
side by side.

In the forest, a native boy went running back to his *pahuichi* and said to his mother: "Down at the village school, mother, the teacher has told us that human beings have five senses."

"What next, my son! Five senses? Take no notice, my child! Forget about it! They say that to deceive us. Just imagine: if that were true, it would not be possible to live."

Another forest boy returned home and, holding out his hand, said, "Look, mother, I've been given this. I'm told that it's called a watch. What am I to do with it?"

"Use it to crack nuts, my son, and keep the quartz. That's the most important thing."

"But mother," protested the child, "in the city, they don't use watches for cracking nuts, they wear them on their wrists and look at them constantly. Why do they keep looking at their watches?"

"Son," replied the mother, "city people don't live like us. Grandfather told me that they ask their watches what they have to do and when they can eat. They have a god called Time, who is linked up to their watches. He speaks to them through their watches and tells them what to do."

"Will he answer me if I ask him?"

"No, my son. Watches don't speak to us because we don't believe in the god Time."

In the Andes, a llama shepherd was playing his quena as he watched his herd walking without haste or fear along the bank of a gentle brook. And the musical silence was suddenly broken: two frontier guards stood aiming modern machine guns at the indigenous shepherd. "Show us your passport!", they shouted.

The shepherd did not know what on earth the men in military uniform were talking about. He decided to explain to them that his parents had also passed by and that, if they did not believe him, they could ask the llamas.

The guards, failing to understand, informed him that it had been decided to confiscate his llamas because he was in a foreign country, ordered him to take four steps backwards and not to cross the frontier that was situated there.

"But what frontier? What is 'frontier'? This is the *Pachamama*."

"The frontier," replied the guards as they traced a line on the dry, sandy ground, "is this line here; to the south, lies our country and to the north, lies yours. You may not cross this line without a passport and a visa."

"But who has told you to draw that line? The *Pachamama* hasn't told us anything about frontiers." Thereupon, with his foot, he rubbed the line out and walked away.

Years later, in that deserted place, a discreet wooden cross stood to show that there somebody had died.

An old man was making his way towards the mountain. That morning, a city youth asked if he could join him.

The old man said to him: "You may come with me. All I ask is that you don't say a word to me as we go along."

The walk began and the youth found it increasingly boring.

"You can rid yourself of as much luggage as you like. In any case, you are free to do what you want."

And the hours went by. Worn out from carrying a heavy rucksack, the youth requested a rest.

"Rest as you walk!" was the reply. The old man then started talking: "If you lack the ability to rest as you walk, you will never reach your goal. Who is forcing you to carry so much weight? Have you brought all that to increase your enjoyment? Is your enjoyment increasing?"

Hours later, the old man and the youth, without his rucksack, were coming to the end of their walk.

"I know that you want to ask me many things," said the old man, "but there is nothing better than silence to understand the teachings of the *Pachamama*.

"Do you want to go on learning? Sit on that rock watching the sunset. If you stay there, a star at twilight will tell you what you need to learn."

"What do you do?" a city woman asked one of my fellow countrymen.

"I'm a shepherd. I tend llamas and alpacas in the mountains," he replied.

"What are you doing here, in the city?"

Villager with young llamas on the shores of Lake Titicaca, Bolivia

"I was curious about it. I wanted to see what the llamas are like down here. But I haven't found any and the people have forgotten to nourish the mountains."

"That is of no importance," retorted the woman. "You can live without llamas and without going to the mountains. We're more modern down here."

"Our parents told us that we should go to the mountains twelve times a year for purification. They also taught us that the llamas and alpacas are there to advise us. I was taught to have patience and to take things calmly. Who teaches the city folk to live serenely?"

And the woman bowed her head and parted in silence.

The vicuna spend the day playing, vicuna have discovered life: they have understood that it is an endless game. Only silly people take it seriously.

"It's dangerous to talk a lot," said the aymara, "because you run the risk of stopping at words."

When modern man realises that words convey only the least important things, he will journey to the frontier of words and become reconciled to silence.

Often, when silence is absent, confusion is present.

And the old man wept; wrapped in silence. It was his first trip to the big city and, sitting opposite a supermarket, he wept, unable to understand why modern man had made everything so complicated.

One of my countrymen approached me and, in a hushed voice, revealed to me a secret that he had discovered when he had lived in the city for a spell: "There, people buy things they don't need, with neither shame nor fear; they hoard things they don't need, with neither shame nor fear; they lie to their brothers, with neither shame nor fear – and, on top of that, they say they're well even if they're not." And, before he left, he whispered to me: "The city dweller lies but he believes in what he says."

It is time to join the *Pachamama*, to discover the immense power stored there, waiting to be released at last. A new world is making ready, the first step towards it must be taken on the pathways of your heart; and preparation entails crowning the art of living through contact with the *Pachamama*.

When you till the land but you do not talk to it; when you take food with no respect for those who patiently and lovingly have provided it; when you build a house without asking the permission of the *Pachamama*; when you do not respect your body; when you soil your mind with selfish thoughts; when, instead of living fully, you debase your existence and convert it into a meaningless routine; when your heart is not an orchard where the trees of love and patience, of enthusiasm and humour, of peace and respect grow; when, in the name of life and in the name of freedom, you fill your life with unhealthy habits and addictions; when, for the sake of gaining time, you find yourself with no time to live; then, brother, perhaps you should stop, call a halt in your life, take a deep breath and look around you: if you stop thinking and renounce haste, a flower or a star will guide your steps and return them to the path of life.

They took our lands from us but they did not succeed in stripping us of our love for the land; they polluted our rivers but they were unable to prevent us from talking about them still. They took away the trees, but the trees' spirits remain, forming invisible woods, encouraging us to go on.

We do not sell our land because the land is our mother; we do not sell the trees because they are our brothers; we do not renounce our ancestral wisdom because we know that, without it, we shall go astray like modern man: the faster he moves, the vaguer is his notion about where he is going.

Before the invasion and the pillage, we were healthy and strong and lived for many, many years. It is not that we were better; it was simply that our steps were unfamiliar with haste and our minds were not subject to brainwashing processes; nor did we eat pleasant-tasting poison or drink sweet, artificially-coloured water.

Now, as then, it is possible to live a healthy life as soon as you stop living with your back turned on nature.

If you have property, you will end up being a slave of what you believe to be your possessions.

In modern society, man is forced to be his own oppressor. It is demanded of us too, the indigenous people, that we join that society; or, to put it another way, that we torture ourselves, that we live with a built-in policeman inside us, that we talk of freedom with the endless clangour of our chains in the background.

We are unbearably free, we are inevitably happy, we are so enthusiastic about living that we cannot stand it.

All my people are farmers. We cultivate food in the soil and our lives in the plot of the existential universe that destiny has seen fit that we plough.

The white man teaches his children to compete but not to share, to vanquish and humiliate his brother. We teach our children to feel nature in its most diverse expression, to love the whole of Creation, to share and to help, to give and to be grateful.

White children play with things that destroy their parents' lives, with machines and weapons. Our children play with flowers and insects, with things that build adults' lives.

There are many festive days on our calendar because those are the days on which the offering of gratitude and respect is made to the *Intij Inti*. A festive day, with its ceremonies and rites, is a communion with the *Pachamama*.

We know that life is the school, nature the classroom and our hearts, the pupils. Our hearts will turn those superb lessons into stories.

Our Forest Community is an experimental centre for the New Alternatives. Our Andes Community is the space for communion with silence.

No, we are not the last; we are the first to set out for the West since the 'discovery' and you can be sure that we intend to stay, so that modern man may understand the eloquence of our silence and the fraternal gesture made by our presence, full and serene like the mountains.

Our forebears were simple men. They neither went hungry nor did they put on weight grotesquely; they did not rush about, nor did they suffer from stress; they walked through life with respect and without fear, feeling that all they were here for was to perform the wonderful task of growth.

We used to be unaware of concepts such as private property and greed; we knew nothing of consumerism and malice. Then they came along and forced us to buy and to sell, to use foreign names and surnames, to feel ashamed of our magic heritage and to forget our rites and tongues.

And now that we have been walking down Western paths for a good few centuries, we are convinced that money does not buy wellbeing, that progress does not enhance the quality of life, that it is both necessary and urgent to give up bad habits and to receive a second education. It is along such a path that we are inviting all our brothers who have been seduced by the West; we are inviting you to a reunion with our sacred, spiritual heritage.

We are the architects of our own lives and of the future which we are building for our children through our crafts.

What about you, Western brother? What are you building?

We are looking for something more than just a moral form of

support for the world's indigenous peoples, the victims throughout history of constant non-understanding.

We know that, until modern man gets to know us properly, he will have no spontaneous feelings of genuine brotherhood.

We are, at one and the same time, the most ancient and the living. We still embody times that are gone, transferring their essence: the seed of things to come.

A concept of life which does not envisage the sacredness of the land is dangerous because it could lead man to commit the most horrific acts of stupidity.

The old teachings of the Andean people are a new contribution that, today, we are ready to make.

We receive nourishment whenever, barefoot, we open our hearts to each dawn: that sublime sensation of life, energy and beauty in the most varied, yet simplest situation.

We are the original discoverers of America; the same thing cannot be discovered twice over. Nor did they discover our cultures. How could other peoples be discovered by those who, as yet, have not even discovered their own roots?

He who moves away from the *Pachamama* lives on the edge of stupidity and suicide.

All we do is meditate; each action is an appointment with respect, and each intention towards the *Pachamama*, a communion.

We are the technique and life is our master.

You, modern men, have a vast external technology, as ineffable as our internal technology. As long as you refuse to work from within, you will run the risk of acting foolishly. There will be a risk that your steps forward will end up as steps into thin air – and you will fall and be buried under the technological waste that, at a time when you were besotted with progress, you insisted on producing.

"The word lies," our ancestors used to say. That is why we must pay greater attention to silence.

As long as hypocrisy lingers in your hearts with impunity, any act will be an empty pantomime and words will inevitably be condemned to rot away on the rubbish dump of meaningless sterility.

Supernatural? What a strange word! Everything is natural, even the things of which man, with his limited vision, is ignorant. The *Pachamama* embraces all, nature knows no limits, there is nothing beyond it, the supernatural does not exist for us.

The indigenous people are merely a point of reference, the living example of the fact that life is something else.

When all those other people were having external, materialistic revolutions, we, the indigenous people, knew that it was not enough to provide people with food, shelter, clothing and work; that what mattered most was missing, often forgotten because we cannot see it with our eyes.

Today, reality has proved us right: it is not possible to forget either our cosmic dimension or our transcendental mission.

We have done our utmost to adapt to Western society. This, however, is beyond the realms of possibility. You have to be stupid and masochistic to live in that society of walking dead men, of hungry corpses, whose only wish is to live to eat and to find amusement in frivolity.

Yes, we have done our utmost, but we cannot dehumanise ourselves. Western brother, it could well be easier for you to become humanised instead and to reconcile yourself to innocence.

And the grandmother is still there, sitting in the nightfall of my memory, serenity adorning her face. As ever, she is clothed in silence, her clear gaze caressing the horizon.

Late afternoon sunlight striking the stone walls of the temple of Sacsayhuaman, above Cuzco, Peru

The *Pachamama* is silent for those of its children who are oblivious of humility. The *Pachamama* likes to hear those of its children who have not reneged on goodness and fraternity, all those who travel along the tracks of reciprocation.

The Amautas used to say that there was a time when essential wisdom was to be found in the trees and the animals. Now it is to be found in all, we know that. Nevertheless, it is sometimes necessary to establish a prior connection with trees and mountains so as to re-establish the connection with our inner wisdom.

In the words of the old aymara, the more you know, the greater the value of silence. Those who are ready to have access to knowledge do not need the teaching to be dressed in words. Those who know little or nothing conceal their ignorance with senseless prattle.

Come! Release your essence and use it to enrich your existence.

If, in going through these teachings, you take a stand above and beyond words, undoubtedly we shall meet and gather together with our ancestors, above and beyond words.

We do not need a permit to say what we feel. It is not necessary to talk a lot; even our silence condemns past genocide and present-day wholesale murder. In spite of it all, as this is a message from the heart of the *Janajpacha*, it is a message of love and fraternity. Our ability to love has not weakened. It is, and we feel that it is, even more pressing and necessary than ever before.

We are innocent and we shall remain so. We shall not make life difficult for ourselves by thinking about what it is to be able to feel; we shall press on down the path, dressed in invulnerability, armed with lucidity, driven by the inexhaustible fuel of love. We are innocent. We are children of the world and we claim the right to innocence for the whole of humanity.

"Brother," said a fellow man, "we want the pollution and the destruction of the *Pachamama* to stop. What will we tell our ancestors when they ask us about it? How will we explain it to our children?"

Perhaps, brother, we should start by decontaminating our minds, for as long as a man considers destruction to be necessary, that man will remain contaminated.

We have come to the West from the nethermost point of our silence to talk to you in the name of fraternity and of life. No, we have not gone mad; we have merely chosen not to mistake life for stupidity.

In Western society, it all boils down to negotiable, profitable goods, from the stupidity of the robot to the pseudo-enlightenment of those who mistake intellectual rubbish for wisdom.

No, brother. We are not going to form part of the city because we do not want to renounce life.

There is no reason why we, the indigenous people, should take up the aberrations of an absurd, superficial world. We will contribute with decisiveness in the destruction of this unbearable situation while sowing the seeds of coming evolution.

No, we are not the only ones; it is just that we have no wish to keep silent in the face of so much generally accepted stupidity.

We know that we are called upon to live a full life and no substitute will stifle our joy for life.

Our brothers were silent, but the stones and the mountains continue to give their wonderful testimony in a language of silence.

Despite the fact that recent history has not been on our side, we shall not give way to hysteria; despite all, we continue to be immersed in the depths of our humility, consciously awaiting the time when we shall no longer be victims but will settle down in the creative present without fear or rancour.

So, here we are, longing for those words which will bring us together in the setting of a refurbished reality.

We are the living remains of the Incario. We shall carry on with the same inner freedom as always.

We renounce continuing beliefs in appearances, the frivolous, meaningless life, selfish individualism, the daily self-deception of surrounding ourselves with objects to conceal inner emptiness, the utterance of dead words, hollow sounds, the evasion of silence; the belief that we know it all, a barren attempt to mask ignorance.

We renounce robotising consumerism, alienating education, dehumanising medicine, the society in which life is what matters least.

We opt for the *Tata Inti* and its route of light, for the *Pachamama* and its path of love, for the full life and its sequence of sublime experiences, the grand ball where the visible and the invisible, the fleeting and the eternal come together.

When we work with our hands, we are meditating.
When we travel, we are meditating.
When we eat, we are meditating.
When we watch the rain, we are meditating.
When we dance, we are meditating;
and the white man comes up to us and asks us
at what time do we do our meditations.

We are farmers and we are ploughing a new furrow in which the seed of the New Andean Man will be able to sprout and grow.

The ways of the Inca Empire live on in our hearts. We are the living part of incomplete history.

As long as man refuses to listen to the voice of other cultures, he will suffer from the most pitiful deafness. He who is incapable of listening to the indigenous people will not be able to hear the voice of the *Pachamama* either.

Frontiers? The *Pachamama* acknowledges no frontiers. We know no limits.

We respect nature and nature protects us.

The purpose of our presence in the West is to provide you with a mirror in which to observe your experiential sequence.

If you have the courage to look inside yourselves, you will be preparing to discover eternity at every instant.

We are of the same religion as the birds and the trees. We know that true religion means liberation because it harmonises with the *Pachamama*.

We are clothed in earth and we can see what is outside as the extension of what remains within.

Our grandparents used to say that death is the return to the *Pachamama*.

"We," said a forest dweller, "carry our umbrellas upside down. We don't understand why the white brother hides from sister rain."

Living for us is a sacred art, a path on which each step bears wisdom.

Where is God?

Brother, it is not possible to see God just like that because he is hidden in every stone, in each drop of water; he walks about in the form of a breeze, playing with the flowers and blowing the mountains into shape.

No, our words are not scientific; they are just true. They are the living testimony of something that is wonderfully real.

We are as important as a stone;
as invulnerable as the wayra;
as serene as the tree;
as silent as the mountain.
We are an experiential space
where all the forces of the Pachamama end.

Remains of village buildings at Machu Picchu, Peru

We have been taught to love our brother, to respect our bodies and minds; to love the plants, the flowers and the stars, the wind and the mountain, a child's smile and an old man's silence.

We have been taught to live without haste or complications.

The *Pachamama* and the *Intij Inti* are the terminological approximation of the unnameable, of what lies way beyond all words and definitions.

You can be sure that, behind these words, God himself is hidden.

The number two is a magic number because it symbolises unity; the number one is likewise magic, because it stands for the essential.

They killed our bodies, distorted our ceremonies but, as we are wayra, air and starlight, the throbbing of essential, millenary knowledge remains intact.

We fulfil ourselves as people and also as a community. It is a breathtaking experience to witness the presence of a constellation of smiles, there between the sky and the earth, with our lives acting as a bridge.

If the future is always absent and the past a canoe borne away by the current, all that remains for us to do is to live the real, eternal present with intensity.

We have seen what is going on in the West and have decided to send over our ancestral heritage so that it may be present in your lives, helping you to change direction.

Western brother, here we are, despite the fact that we were mowed down by history; here we are, telling you that we are going to build a different future in which we will all shake hands.

We, the indigenous people, work with love and enthusiasm. That is why we take holidays without stopping work.

It was said in the forest that city folk have lost the ability to know when it is time to eat; they ask a strange thing that they wear on their wrists and, every time they look at it, they hasten their steps.

A doctor was giving his advice to an old man, saying, "It is not good for the stomach to fill it with animals. Find a scientific reason why it is not good to eat meat!"

"It is not good," said the old man, "of course, it is not good. How could it be good? We know that it is not good, it is not good ... for the animals."

The grandfather's granddaughter was a student in the city and, during the holidays, she would come and visit the community. One day, the teenage granddaughter complained of a severe headache. The eighty-year old grandfather reacted immediately: "Do not tell a lie, my dear, the head never aches."

We were leaving a meeting at which people of all sorts had made an exception in their lives and established a space for reflection, listening closely to the thoughts of the ever-decreasing indigenous people. At the end of the meeting, a man told us firmly: "What I dislike about you people is that you're right."

And the old man said that goods become bad when you start hoarding them.

And the indigenous people refused to live on the second floor.

"It is too far from the earth," they said, "it is like turning our backs on the *Pachamama*. We have to be close to the earth, to be able to feel it; to be high up, we are sorry to say, is detrimental."

When we have a problem, we sing and dance – and in the middle of the dance, we catch sight of the solution.

Nature is the temple awaiting your return.

And the old man carried a huge stick. "It helps you up," he said, "and it helps you down. It is neither good nor bad. It all depends on the way you've decided to go."

And my countryman looked surprised as he watched a heavy smoker. Smoking is a ritual component for sacred and occasional use; the smoke forms the visible bridge to the invisible dimension.

Gateway at Sacsayhuaman, Cuzco, Peru

And they told him a lot about a machine to look out for. He was a young man, bursting with curiosity. He left the forest and went to the city. In a city not far from the forest, a forest dweller watched with great attention a machine that was washing clothes. The young man returned, saying that he had found the machine they had told him so much about. "Life looks better without a machine," he said.

"I talk to the stones," said an old man on the outskirts of a city, "because they are always willing to listen. I always carry a stone with me so that I may talk to it when I have not been understood. In talking to it, I find protection from those who talk to me so much that they could reconcile me to speculation. The stone protects me. It is the symbol of my mountain, the visible part of my invisible inner mountain."

Western brother, what are you waiting for? Warm yourself by the indigenous fire of our aching heart, now that we have come to you.

When I dip my foot into the river, when I caress a flower or emptiness, when I sit on the mountain top or persistently think of tomorrow, it is then that I sense, Western brother, your future and mine as brethren in a unifying present.

When I go down to the cities and I see that you are absent, I long for you constantly and bring you, yet again, his urgent message.

Brother, each one is responsible for this opportunity offered by the immense potential given to him. Live!

Although it is not obvious, the indigenous message is present like an incandescent flame, calling you to a different future.

"No, brother," said the elder. "This is not a hallucination. This is a city." Their occupation? Dreamers, adapting pressing dreams to different realities.

We can contribute to humanity only by walking the world clothed in humility.

And the doctor of the Andes said to the indigenous traveller that life is a journey at every instant; if you stop, you lose your bearings; if you cling on to things, you tire and you don't get very far; each step contains its goal and each opportunity is a vein from which you can learn so much about the wonderful art of growing.

Life is a journey, it begins with the decision to approach the canoe, the fragile vessel that will enable you to make it to the other shore of reality, to a life of quality, standing beyond the tempest that was raging when you set off on this transcendental journey.

And the forest dwellers laughed. They were working, but it looked more like a party. A foreign researcher took one look and left. "Those savages must be, drunk or crazy," he thought. About the white man they had seen, the forest dwellers said: "He must be ill because there is no smile on his face, or perhaps he's a born fool and misses out on everything in life."

I have a pile of problems. What can I do? Perhaps they're messages, perhaps just opportunities; dance in silence at dusk and you will see how the way out appears clearly before you.

"Mother," said a forest child, "Why aren't we born with shoes like the white man?" "Son, it must be because we don't need them. Grandfather says that, if it were necessary, we would have been born with shoes on – like the white man."

"Mother," said another forest child, "I want to go and see the city from where the world comes to an end."

"That's all right, my child, but don't let anybody see you, and don't look for too long because it will hurt your eyes."

"The city trees have left," explained an old man in the forest, "because the white man has not respected them; the animals have died and the earth has turned into a desert; the rivers no longer offer advice and the mountains complain. I have asked the stars and they've told me that they are all are calling on man to return to the big house, where there is neither sickness nor hunger."

And the priests chased my people from the forest – so as to dress them and to teach them that it is shameful and immoral to walk about naked. Now, many forest dwellers dress, they feel ashamed of their bodies and they commit sexual offences that never before had been seen in their communities.

"Please," begged a Guarani Indian of his master, "I don't want a holiday."

"But we are bound by law to let you rest," was the reply.

"But, in working, we rest," said other Indians who had gathered round.

And that fellow countryman, finding himself in the forest of jaguars and leopards, climbed a leafy tree where, so as to keep out of the way of the wild cats, he decided to spend the night. On the following morning, he looked to the right and he looked straight ahead to find two wild cats keeping him company. They had spent the night in the same tree.

At that instant, the man remembered the old man's teachings: "Animals do no harm, they just defend themselves when we attack them." He calmly climbed down the tree and went on his way silently – watched closely by the two wild cats as they began their day.

And the old man wept. A foreign researcher approached him and asked him why he was weeping. The old man stood up and, as the tears ran down his face, charged: "Why aren't you crying? Can't you hear the wailing earth and the sobbing trees? Why aren't you crying? For how much longer will the city dweller remain deaf?"

And the old man went on weeping disconsolately.

My people pay the greatest attention to what goes on both inside and outside themselves, what goes on in their bodies, what goes through their minds, what goes before their eyes, the invisible seen with the inner eye.

Make your home into a sacred place; your body into a sacred

place; your mind into a sacred place; your entire planet into a sacred place; and the sense of the sacred will arouse the other senses that are still dormant.

An Andean was invited to dinner at a house in the city. And the meal began, the dishes were passed with total indifference, just like lies dressed in sincerity. Some of the guests regretted that the Andean had no table manners: he didn't know how to use a knife and fork, or drink champagne.

The dinner was over, the guests, heaving with indigestion, had left; the Andean guest had thoroughly enjoyed himself; no, he didn't know about knives and forks; his parents had only taught him, to enjoy his food.

And when the Andean was getting ready to sleep in the square, a woman called to him from her house: "You can't sleep there! There are people about!" She invited him to sleep in her house and the Andean was taken to a room and the bed in which he would sleep that night.

The next day, the devout woman went to the Andean's room to find him sleeping on the floor. "This bed is the place to sleep," she said. "Have you slept on the floor all night?" And the Andean replied: "I slept on and off, whenever I got down on the floor, but I also used the bed occasionally – to ponder."

"We are not born complete," explained a man from the Southern Andes. "We come to this life for that very purpose: completion."

Before joining the community and being accepted as fully-fledged men, young Andeans must pass the relevant initiatory tests. The toughest test consists of crossing the Andes to the East and returning with something from the plains that lie where the mountains end.

Hunger, thirst, cold and prolonged solitude and darkness can be overcome only when the wayfarer has a will of stone, making him invulnerable, and an alert mind, enabling him to watch every step with a total absence of fears and misgivings.

Street scene, Buenos Aires, Argentina

Photo: Mark Edwards/Still Pictures

125

He who does not pass this test, does not return. He who does not return – it is of no matter, there is no point in having incomplete people.

And the Incas crowned their feet in sandals of gold, symbolising the steps on the way to the Sun, the route of boundless lucidity. The Incas warned those who attached great importance to the head to be careful: it is thus that many are lost and fall into the abyss of speculation.

In the Southern Andes, the young shepherds learn to be on the alert from the moment they learn to walk; their alertness is sharpened as they go along with their fathers and the flock. The indigenous people know that wild cats come only when the shepherd is asleep, abandoned to lost thoughts. They know that the wild cat comes and carries off an animal when the shepherd lets his guard down. Then, on seeing the animal being carried off, he remains motionless and gives himself a scolding. He forgives himself and learns. You cannot go through life with your eyes closed, you must understand; assume a different attitude as he who understands the teaching the first time round.

He who is guided by his head lives a life of division, with his heart agonising in its wake. He who makes an unbreakable union of head and heart lives a life of harmony.

"We come from the gods," said a forest dweller, "and, here on earth, we must prepare ourselves for the day when we shall again become transparent gods.

"We come from the stars and to the stars we return, up the path of the mountain from whose pinnacle we shall, one day, perhaps tomorrow, appear dressed in light and transparency and, from that moment, we shall help you in your pilgrimage."

And a landed millionaire had bought a piece of land in the forest. When he saw that the forest people were in the habit of embracing the trees, he announced that those who wished to embrace the trees would have to work half a day every day on his ranch. From that day onwards, every morning, a group of forest people worked in silence on the ranch until midday, when they ran off to embrace their friends who, in motionless green, waited each day for that hour of that day.

Years later, the landowner decided to sell the trees to the timber dealers. And, one after another, they fell. Close by, hidden in the foliage, several dozen eyes looked on from behind a pane of tears, in a deep silence broken only by electric saws, as the trees were felled.

Another landowner, rolling in fat, all diets having failed, looked afraid and mistrusting at a silent forest dweller. "What can he be thinking about when he doesn't speak?" he thought. "What can he be up to when, at night, he sits by the fire or gazes up at the stars?

Why doesn't he tire or feel thirsty? Why doesn't he complain? Why doesn't he speak and why does he walk barefoot on the ground?

Why does he dance at dawn? Why does he speak in silence? Why doesn't he fear death? Why, when he stares at me, do I have the feeling that he's looking through me? Why does his presence put me on edge, just like his absence?

Why does he appear before me, even in my dreams, as if, in his silence, he were claiming something from me? Why does his silence make me feel ill?"

A landowner, his head in his hands, crying and, nearby, a forest dweller – watching.

Sunrise over stone on the shores of Lake Titicaca

CHAPTER FOUR

The Cosmic Vision
of the Andean Shamans

"What can I do to be healed?" people ask. *Wasimasillay:* all you have to do is put silence in your minds, silence in your bodies, thus allowing your inner shaman to act. All you have to do is to leave him at peace, being at peace.

Despite not believing in energy nor knowing how to handle it, a doctor can help or hinder, in the belief that he is doing good. But, how much more help could be afforded by a therapist capable of channelling the energy of the *Pachamama*? A therapist who, in his wisdom, would understand therapy as self-therapy, commencing the instant that something starts happening within the patient, like the rumbling of a volcano as it releases its transforming energy, on its way to life and its wonderful immenseness.

What we are proposing is simply the return to our natural state, hand in hand with the *Pachamama*, dressed as a flower, a star, a butterfly, a cloud or a sunrise. Shamanism, brother, consists of simply moving closer to our origins, heart in hand.

Have you discovered that there is a teaching attached to everything, that life is the best school, full of invisible masters guiding your steps? The invisible clothes itself in the visible so as to help you.

See how the air embraces the earth, how the wind blows the mountains into shape and caresses the flowers.

See how the clouds shed tears of joy and the trees provide

you with oxygen and food; see how the birds sing of their gratitude day by day and how the spring bursts forth with happiness.

This is the festivity of life that some people have not yet realised.

Do not value only what you do, value also what you do not do. The way to the mountain is sacred from start to finish.

Spread your wings and fly to the pinnacle of your freedom. A secret will show you the flight path: dare yourself to do it! Daring is the magic formula.

The best way to start flying is – to fly.

You are a condor.

How do trees teach?

Change into a bird and, when you return from your flight, you will hear the voice of the old tree, the mouthpiece of ancestral wisdom. Only those who embark on the upward flight find the language of the *Pachamama*.

It all comes down to attaining our natural state at a natural pace – naturally. This is the essence of Andean shamanism.

Harmonise with the Universe and its limitless protection will come to you. Trust the *Pachamama* and the *Pachamama* will rise with you each morning.

When the wayfarer sets off on his journey, he becomes its sacred being.

And the Amautas built the paths and opened their travelling school in the middle of the woods, barefoot, feeling every single step. The Amauta spoke with interludes of silence while the group of disciples walked behind, listening, feeling. It was all accounts and silence along those circular paths.

When you move on aimlessly, when you feel and do not bother to think, when your feet converse with our brothers the birds in their symphony, the Amautas' accounts form part of the landscape and of constant learning, the purpose and the reason behind this journey.

A Basque boy had wandered into the forest and lost his bearings. One day, after many days of walking hither and thither, he found a way, a path that was scarcely visible and followed it with great excitement. The hours went by, a whole night, a short rest and then, the next day, on with the task.

His hopes were renewed by seeing some footprints: "I'll follow the footprints," the Basque said to himself. Hours later, he began to see more and more footprints. They seemed to belong now to two people, now to three. In some places, the countryside seemed familiar to him – "Perhaps I've been here before," he thought. Further on, he discovered that the footprints looked like his own and he mused: "Perhaps they belong to other Basques walking ahead of me."

Some time later, our Basque friend realised that he was going round and round on the same path. It was one of the few remaining Amauta circular paths. They were once used by the travelling schools of our forefathers.

I spend my life suffering from one sickness after another," a man complained.

"Learn the shamanic art!"

"How can I learn something so complicated?"

"The shamanic life style," the Amauta continued, "consists of simply living to the full, walking invulnerably through life, living the instant guided by the instinct. Did I hear you say 'complicated'? It is the return to the human being's natural state! To go on living in confusion, with no inner power, in the hope that you're healthy – well, that's what I call 'complicated'!"

In many cases, it is difficult to acknowledge that what you know, diplomas included, serves only to prolong ignorance.

"Why do you spend so much time meditating?" the old man was asked.

"Meditating doesn't mean doing nothing. For us, meditation means a departure from the world so as to journey through the *Janajpacha*, gather with our forebears, with wise men from other cultures. It means merging into the Universe and gaining direct access to a huge mound of information; finding different resources with which to help others and to continue vibrating in harmony with the cosmos. Andean meditation is the sacred journey that we undertake in different ways; it is access to complete freedom, where you retrieve your state of limitlessness."

"What happens to the body when you meditate?"

"The body is the husk of the seed; the body just waits in a deep state that many people may mistake for temporary bodily death; and the return is a rebirth."

Why do people become ill? Illness should not be interpreted as something negative. On the contrary, it should be taken as a space for reflection in which the person has the chance to take a look at himself and his environment. It is the right time for self-observation, for seeing, for feeling each of our steps and the direction in which they are moving.

Illness often acts as a mere messenger showing us the way we should not take, the way of life we should renounce. Illness is a chance to return to the great house, to the cosmos.

In practising profound silence, you prepare yourself for vibrating in unison with the *Pacha* (Universe) and for tuning into cosmic wisdom denied to those who live like slaves to their five senses and their intellect. Tune into the cosmos and you will discover that all is energy, that is, love.

The terraces of Machu Picchu with the mountain of Putucusi beyond

"What do I need to feel well?"

"All you need to do is find your place, your spot, your centre in the cosmos. When this occurs, a spring of wellbeing will burst forth within you."

"How can I achieve it?"

"It is part of our natural state to be able to do so, just as swimming in the water is the natural state of the fish. All you have to do is evolve into a flower, a mountain, a star, *Pachamama*. Silence is the method, and humility the requirement."

"How can I know whether I'm tuned into the *Pachamama*?"

"When you feel an uncontrollable desire to love, then you are vibrating in unison with the *Pachamama*. Remember that love, as our master *T'unupa* taught us, is unconditional, free of demands and fears, free of addictive relationships and dependence. Love is access to true freedom. Freedom without love is dangerous.

"We know that thought and intention have a lot of power. Take care of what you think and you'll find a great ally; neglect it and you'll be the first victim.

"When you settle down in the cosmos, your limitations vanish and you become all.

"The invisible communities are the Andean people's reserve of wisdom and lucidity. Gradually, they are starting to come forward and to show that living can be different."

A crisis, be it an illness or a social conflict, is not just a problem but essentially a chance to start a new stage. Many people do not value their health, some even go so far as to lose it. However, if we are able to face things in the right way, that momentary illness will enable you to rediscover not only health but also the transcendental meaning of life. When circumstances are critical, it all depends on the direction in which we set our steps. Remember that, when you make up your mind to move forward, the entire Universe, all of *Pachamama*, is with you.

No, it is not that modern man is absolutely wrong. However, an incomplete, fractional vision of reality can lead one to think that reality is only what is known – that is, a tiny part. This, in turn, leads to an absurd way of life, bereft of inner power.

We must resume our vision of the *Janajpacha* to realise that here there is more, and that precisely those things that are ignored officially are the most important.

You will be able to discover more things, gradually or suddenly, by including in your life silence and momentary solitude, periodic fasts, occasional music and dance, or a simple walk barefoot through the woods, stopping now and then to embrace the trees. From the outset, this will make you sensitive and receptive, enabling you to feel the language of the *Pachamama*.

The rest is indescribable and cannot be expressed in words.

How is it possible to live disconnected from the source of cosmic energy, cut off in the world of the synthetic, boxed in by intellectual concepts, all of which prevent us from living fully with power and miracles?

How is it possible to use the word, 'life' about the grotesque, senseless existence now prevailing in the modern Western world?

I think I understand those who commit suicide: it is not possible to go on living like that. Nonetheless, suicide is a false alternative. The alternative to suicide is total transformation, but this requires greater courage, in the sense that it is an ongoing task of self-observation in the midst of a storm of criticism and advice.

Transformation is the passage leading to the *Janajpacha*. It should entail a profound change as opposed to mere superficial modifications that are no substitute for deep, total change.

All you have to do is trust yourself; the *Pachamama* takes care of everything else. However, only he who loves his own self is able to trust. If you are willing to love yourself, then you are capable of looking after your body, your attitudes, your thoughts and your feelings.

Make your contribution with decisiveness and courage and the doors of the *Pachamama* will open wide.

"The mountains were our refuge yesterday," recalled the old man. "Today they are our reference point. From them, we learned invulnerability, constancy, serenity, the meditative attitude; the mountain and our own selves are no longer two different things, the mountain is inside us and we are inside the mountain."

The knowledge that at the end of the day comes night, that at the end of this life comes death, should encourage us to make the best use of each day, living each and every instant to the full.

He who lives profoundly stands beyond death; he discovers eternity as it flows along disguised as fleetingness.

We know that it might be considered bad manners to stay awake in a country where it is customary to remain asleep. It is, nevertheless, essential to wake up so as not to mistake the apparent for true reality. By awaking, you are liberated from routine and imposed conditioning; by awaking, you open the door to profound life.

What does living mean? Living is the return to the *Pachamama*, to the great house, in order to drink again from the inexhaustible fountain of wisdom and be capable of communicating permanently with the cosmos. Living is the discovery that you are not alone, that you never have been, that you are life, bound ultimately for eternity.

In a society which dehumanises and robotises from childhood, it is our duty to remain firmly anchored in the everlasting lucidity that is incarnate in day-to-day experiences. Completeness is the vaccination against stupidity and insignificance.

Do not cling desperately to anything. Just make sure that the ways that lead to you and your depths are clear, free of the obstacles of the intellect and the stones of reason. Then, when you are able to go down into your depths, you will discover the true expression and power of the *Pachamama*, waiting, today as yesterday, for us to rediscover it.

Are you alive? The ability to love unconditionally is the way to show that we are truly alive.

The 'dead' do not love; they just trade in feelings and actions and, when the deal does not work out, they complain and become frustrated, angry and violent. The 'dead' have a bad time of it because they have turned their backs on life.

The old man stood watching the night fall, motionless like the mountain; later, in the presence of the stars, around a tree did he slowly walk; not a thought passed through his mind, for he had become a tree or a star and, occasionally, he took clear flight.

Where do we go when we die?

You will know that when you know where your steps are going, before you die. It is before death that you must know which way your steps are going because, on dying, you will find a ready-made route.

Until you start trusting yourself, you will not be able to trust the *Pachamama*; until you start trusting the *Pachamama*, the door to your cosmic dimension will remain closed.

The wise tree once told me that, if the human being fails to understand his mission on earth, he will not only cause harm to his own self but will also block the path of evolution of those other species whose purpose it is to help him.

Settle down in the cosmos, lie back in the arms of the Universe and, from there, embrace your brother. An embrace is therapy enough when we are in tune with the *Pachamama*.

That evening at twilight, they buried the grandmother who had died 'accidentally' after being accused by the village priest of being in touch with the devil. The Andean grandmother did not understand what company she was being accused of keeping, because she had always lived alone.

Much to the doctors' dismay, the grandmother had been able to cure those who were considered scientifically to be incurable.

"If you really want to live, you will get better," she would tell her patients as she performed her therapeutic ritual, the way to return to a state of health.

Every day at dusk, the grandmother would go out and talk to a stone.

The day then came when, at the usual time, she came out of her home in a coffin. A rough tombstone marked the spot where the grandmother was buried. There, in silence, a stone took up residence. It was removed time and time again, and yet, it kept coming back. Not far from the tomb, the stone that the grandmother used to talk to had disappeared.

And the Quechuan elder carried away a dying youth who had been thrown out of hospital with the advice: "Go home and die!"

The elder happened to be passing and, on hearing this, took the youth to his home leaving the doctors' contemptuous words behind him.

Months later, an old man and a healthy, robust youth entered the hospital to offer their greetings to the very doctors who, not long before, had said that the youth's days were numbered. After the usual procedure with the stethoscope, all the doctors together, amazed by the youth's vigour, declared that the cure was not scientific.

The doctor is the warrior,
the warrior, the poet,
the poet, the master,
the master, the musician,

the musician, the shaman,
the shaman, the human being
releasing his inner potential.

On the sacred way to the conquest of the inner mountain, there is no pre-determined order; each individual finds his own way of moving on.

The normal perception of reality is the dream from which you must awake. Frequently, the dreams that come before an awakening are the most conflictive ones.

According to Andean tradition, little dreams are to be forgotten, while big dreams can shed light on to your path because they are part of the other reality.

Modern man needs to re-channel his energies and give his vision a new focus. When he starts to sense the immense power within him and uses the inner eye, he will see that all is infinite.

The snake sheds its skin to remind us that we must be reborn; the chicken breaks its shell and hatches out to *Jatunwasi*, reminding us of our chance to move into the other reality.

Opening your heart is like breaking the shell that enables you to establish direct contact with the *Pachamama*. To open your heart is to escape from the prison of the intellect and to settle into your cosmic dimension.

When you unite your own inner fire with that of the *Pachamama*, you will come into contact with a powerful transforming force which will enable you to install an everlasting light in your heart.

The deeper you go into the cosmos, the more you will grow; the more you grow within, the more your body will turn into a body of light until it becomes transparent and invisible.

Let your *lantin* show through.

Our altar is invisible. Would you like to see it? The tree trunk is the visible manifestation of the invisible.

Andean shamanism brings a message of hope and life, a life style in which, despite all the problems, everything is harmony.

We are aware of our limitations, but we are also aware of the great potential within us. We know that, although Andean shamanism is not a panacea, it is nonetheless a wonderful different opportunity to attain a life of transcendent quality.

Go! Climb the sacred mountain! That is the route of purification. When you reach the top, you will find the magic cavern from which you may approach the other reality.

The circle is the basic form of the Universe. All is circular and cyclical. The circle is sacred and, with the fire inside, we re-create the essential form of the *Pachamama*.

"Since the times of our ancestors," said the old man, "we have been in contact with the condor. The condor is the sacred bird that shows us the way to go; the condor is the constant reminder that we can fly high above. Fly, fly up! You are a condor!"

Being a condor means that you have your own built-in lift.

Far from being an unwholesome habit, smoking is part of the ritual, for occasional use. Smoke symbolises access to the *Janajpacha*, the visible bridge to invisible reality.

No, brother, this is not a panacea; it is our testimony.

We are merely the forerunners of old Andean experiences.

And one day, it happened that the voice of the mountain called on me to fulfil a mission. It was then that I took the Andean seed and went off one night in search of the fertile soil of human hearts.

When you meditate, look to the East;
when you dance, dance barefoot;
when day breaks, be up to await the Sun;
when you speak to the Pachamama,
harbour no doubts, your words shall be heard.

140

Everything in the *Pachamama* is a symbol that our ancestors taught us to decipher with respect.

Nature is a poem and the shaman is the poet who takes his existence for a walk amid verses visible to the eye or to the heart.

Andean shamanism requires a deep level of purification because its purpose is to commune with the Universe. In Andean shamanism, the shaman's role consists of helping you to live more fully and freely, to link up with your inner shaman; the rest is mere superstition.

When you think, you become united with the *Pachamama* and you discover your eternity. Inner silence is the best way to establish contact with the inner universe.

The silence of the mountain will imbue you with serenity and humility. When you return, you will see that a mountain has risen within you; it is the stairway to the *Janajpacha*, the door to the other reality.

A genuine therapist relates to the patient in such a way that each becomes part of the other. There is no one better than oneself to know what needs to be done.

Cells are the stars of our bodily universe. Your clarity and brightness can be enhanced by eating plain food and forging a balanced mental attitude.

Andean shamanism offers you the chance to start a new life, to set off on the way back to the natural state, to your origin, to the *Jatunwasi*, to the *Pachamama*. To put it in a nutshell, the shamanic attitude consists of living the present moment to the full.

The shaman's work is fundamental: through therapy and ritual, the aim is to establish contact with the inner shaman dwelling in all hearts. Once this connection has been made, the therapy changes into self-therapy.

A trance? We are talking about inspiration and connection, of fusion and of access to the other dimension. We play with the

Pachamama and we do so because we want to, we find enjoyment in what we do. Nobody forces us to do it, it is not a heavy burden that we are expected to shoulder; we do not feel possessed by anything other than life and its delightful sequence of opportunities.

We do not feel bad when something goes wrong: the outcome never depends solely on our effort or our wishes. Very often, we do things that people consider to be miracles, but this, for us, is like a game for a child. We are not used to being applauded or approved of by anybody. All that we do within the shamanic attitude forms part of the existential vocation known as life.

Once, we were told that all we had to do was live and we believed it.

And, dressed in brightness, we are walking down a limitless, timeless path, in tune with the Universe; following the route of Andean shamanism. There we go, free without punishment, happy beyond bearing, irreversibly human. Are you coming?

If you fail to find enjoyment throughout your journey, you will be missing life in its most beautiful sense.

All of us, including you, have the duty to
grow day by day.
To grow, all you need to do is keep awake.

To live without essential knowledge is like going off to war with a chocolate machine gun.
Andean shamanism prompts you to convert what you know into an intense experiential sequence. If you don't do it, the mud of incoherence will make a shipwreck of your power.

Why do you waste your energy on nonsense when you don't even have enough to discover life?

Talk to your food before you eat it,
to the mountain before you climb it,

Staircase and entrance door to the Pyramid Temple of Kalasasaya, Tiwanaku, Bolivia

to your body and the stars,
to the dawn and your inner shaman;
they all sense you.
Many will help you find the path of life.

You are never alone from the minute you start to move forward
hand in hand with the *Pachamama*. The gateway to the other reality
stands in your heart. You will find it by travelling to the shores of
reason, where the stairway to the other dimension awaits you. By
travelling to our origins, we conquer the present and we shall
embody a different future.

And when you feel yourself to be a flower, a mountain, a dawn, you
will no longer be afraid of forgetting or of going down the sacred path.
You will reach full life, surrounded by all those dead beings who
wander the streets; you will see life as an unequalled opportunity, as a
wonderful gift and you will drink in each day as if it were sweet wine.

And when you go back into the cosmos, and you feel yourself to
be the forest, the waterfall, the dusk, you will realise that it is not
worth wasting days and energy on thought and doubts or of
fostering rancour, and you will hand your life over in favour of
life; reconciling a strict discipline to the enthusiasm of he who
walks, free of stress and trivia, to the celebration of life. You are
still in time to go through life happily.

On leaving the world, you learn to live in it; but if you persist in
complicating matters and feel the need for many things, then you
have not yet left the world and your steps are not moving in the
supreme direction.

Some people mistake going camping for leaving the world. This
is tantamount to mistaking, a stone for bread, and eating the stone.

When you reconcile attitude and intention in a setting of
coherent vibration, each of your actions acquires power;

appearances crumble and the essence shows through; you sense your eternity and assume your sublime freedom.

Empty your head of all those mounds of information; reconcile yourself to silence and, when you stand before yourself, open up to the *Pachamama*; place your problems and facts and figures in the hands of the *Pachamama*; and then you will begin to see and understand that seeing is more than what eyes can show you and you will ride over and above appearances.

If a man with inner power asks for rain, it rains because the clouds obey him. A man of power is simply one who has made the sun come out in his heart and who lives in a state of dawn even when the day is over.

We rise to the *Janajpacha* with the help of invisible assistants; everything works communally, even the things that the ordinary eye fails to see.

The first step is to change the window through which you look out on to your daily reality. The other window is the access to freedom, to a different mentality, capable of effortlessly controlling what would otherwise have to be channelled. The other window is the new perception, beyond all routine and normal situations.

Another fundamental step consists of abolishing fears in a thorough, radical way; there is nothing more beautiful than facing adversity in a state of freedom, acting with determination and spontaneity, embodying fervent humility.

And my countryman sank into a long silence. "What are you doing?" he was asked. "I'm listening to myself and, when necessary, I travel to any sick part of my body and, with the energy of the *Pachamama*, I make it whole again."

"I am entitled to be bored," the old man said, "but I don't exercise my right." When you live with inner power, everything is interesting – and possible.

"We withstand the freezing cold," said one of my countrymen, "because, at will and depending on our needs, we can send blood and warmth all through our bodies." And anybody can do this.

Purify yourself by climbing the mountain on an empty stomach and alone; plunge into the silence of quality and, when you return, you will be able to hear the voice of our brother the wood, calling to you and holding out his hand.

For as long as you are not dead, live! Release the power that lies within you; you don't need to think a lot or remain a slave to reason; you don't need to be clear about everything or fight in the enemy trench. Live!

Living means accepting your circumstance with enthusiasm and courage, decisiveness and patience; change it, you are a being with power and this, you must never forget. Live!

Don't let yourself be seduced by the past or the future; throw yourself into each step; each day, this could be your final act – and that does not matter either because death is the dawn of another day, of that day which, one day, will come into your life. But today, live!

The twilight of your life has not come yet. Live! It is a matter of urgency that you live, fully.

In Andean shamanism, we say that only the strong love, those who live the present, those who are free and do not smother the freedom of others; those who, expecting nothing, give all, even their lives, theirs is the only superior way – of living.

We are at once here and in the *Janajpacha*. We control and flow, we are attentive and relaxed; we have everything and we cling to nothing; we trust in our own selves because we are part of something big; nothing catches us off our guard, for us, a surprise is a source of enjoyment and learning.

We are invulnerable like the wind; we are like water, we have renounced all and feel that we lack nothing. Power is the point of reference, and magic the door that closes on those who don't know what it's all about.

Andean shamanism is the therapy of transformation; the cure cannot be performed in this reality alone.

If you have not discovered the art of living, then you are not completely awake; if your life does not flow naturally, sickness will still knock on your door.

Remember, you are a multi-dimensional being and life is a wonderful opportunity.

A drum, a maraca and a toy, a stone, a flower and the fluttering wings of silence, a cave and a dawn, a profound intention and the vocation for growing are the right setting, in which to go over to the other side, to the shores of this multi-dimensional reality.

Visualisation is shamanic in origin; our visualisation begins with deep concentration. He who is able to concentrate his mind is well on the way to handling power.

And the voice of the tree helped me understand the message of the mountain.

You will recognise a shaman when he who presents himself as such is the embodiment of the shamanic attitude; when his presence, even when silent, dressed in humility, reaches your inner depths.

The journey begins by looking this reality in the face. If you cannot reach this point with lucidity or move through it with unshakeable calm, how can you hope to cross to the other shore? While you refuse to look your everyday life in the face, the other reality will be a mere excuse for the inability you yourself have chosen. You will begin to sense the other reality when you start working on your way of perceiving things.

Without a firm intention and deep concentration, every action carries the risk of going in the wrong direction, like a wasted chance.

To fast is to come to the aid of your consciousness, especially when fasting includes the abandonment of thought.

If you are bound by chains, your inner shaman can break them; if fears linger, the *Pachamama* can deal with them. Never forget that nature has endowed you with the ability to work miracles.

Andean shamanism does not expect to be believed or to be a question for debate; it is to be experienced and felt. It is only with a shamanic attitude that you will be able to see the revelation of power; to be on the outside looking in is like trying to thread a needle in the dark.

If you do without your sight and set the inner eye to work, you will be able to see with your entire body; if you work hard on your eye, you will be able to see clearly.

When you live with the shamanic attitude, your body is filled with light, and a guardian spirit, in the form of a tree, a star or an animal, will be with you till the end of the road.

If you accept only one reality, you will find shamanic attitudes absurd. Andean shamanism is something more than magic, it is an appointment with a different state of consciousness; it is the stairway to the *Janajpacha*; the bridge to the other science.

Shamanism is just another way, simple and profound; it is the return to our natural state – naturally.

With the shamanic attitude, the bridge between the sky and the earth is built; that wonderful bridge is, in fact, people, coherent people.

By releasing the power that lies within you and finding your centre in the *Pachamama*, you take up residence in the *Chej-Pacha* and you burst out into unbridled joy as you perceive that all is unity, all is life and eternity.

If you still see things as separate units, you need to travel to the magic cavern of your inner mountain. If you forget that each day is another rung in your evolution, it could be that you are still walking down the wrong path.

But do not worry! If you redirect your steps, today, as yesterday, the *Pachamama* will be awaiting your arrival. Are you coming? Welcome to life!

Come! Let's make the invisible visible! Let's unite the sky with the earth and, in silence, let's set our vibrations as one.

And the caterpillar is there, beside the butterfly, hoping that each one will take the choice when his turn comes.

When you tune into the *Pachamama*, you see eternity behind fleetingness; you acquire awareness of the meaning of your life and of the meaning of each day.

The shamanic attitude takes us into the invisible community of hearts, the invisible convergence of intentions. For those who want to arrive, the door will not be open for much longer.

And the unknown becomes known; the supernatural becomes natural and the temporary, eternal. Andean shamanism is the debunking of the impossible.

A ritual? The first ritual in which you should take part is your daily life, where each action and intention turn into the expression of the sacred and of power and of the delightful task of growing.

Be careful! The minute your attention wanders, you will fall into the clutches of words; words that, in the form of subtle traps, will prevent you from attaining experience, when life is nothing more than pure experience. Some people are extremely learned about everything – except living.

When you plunge into the ocean of Andean shamanism, time unites with eternity, your circumstance with immensity, cosmic potential with your personal circumstance.

Each individual sets his own limits until, one day, he discovers that we are limitless.

First, learn to live here; the rest is reserved for those who have found real life.

When you are able to control your dreams at will and make

your life into something more beautiful than a dream; when your hands can see without touching and your eyes know without seeing; when you feel that all is one; that illness does not form part of the natural state but often of transcendental learning; when you stop forgetting that you are part of immenseness; and when, behind each man, you see a chance for evolution, then you will have set your steps on the way of the sacred tradition.

Andean shamanism is the ancestral invitation to transcendental life, to an experiential sequence set in the immensity of the cosmos. Are you coming?

Come! Let us blend into the condor and fly! Let us soar to the pinnacle of freedom.

Where does Andean shamanism lead? To the dimension – the poetic dimension.

And an ancestral message, sent by the gods, has arrived in your heart. In fact, it is an invitation to travel to a place where, this time, your body is of no use.

This book is an excuse for us to meet beyond the word, in a place where I await you, sitting on an intention.

And the timeless voice said: "I have come to share my Utopia with your freedom because the time has arrived for unconditional love."

What about fanning the flames of happiness until enthusiasm settles with impunity in everybody's heart? What about nurturing serenity until it blossoms in our consciousness? How would it be if you took charge of this task, without further ado? Let the shamanic light enlighten you and the *Tata Inti* walk beside you.

CHAPTER FIVE

A Quechuan Prayer

Pachi Pachamama,
Imaraycuchus ricusayku caipicainiykita,
P'achallisqa p'isqomanta,
sut'iyaimanta Urq'manta.
Pachi asirihuasqaykurayku
chay ashka chaupi t'ika ukhumanta.
Pachi, imaraycuchus ch'inkayniykiwan
sapa chisiyaspa yachachiwaiku:
"Wajchakayqa, nan winay Janajpachaman"
Pachi kay k'acha kutimanta.

Thank you, *Pachamama,*
because we feel
your presence, dressed as a bird,
a mountain or a dawn;
thank you for smiling at us
through flowers of many colours;
thank you because, in silence,
you show us each nightfall.
"Humility is the way to eternity".
Thank you for this wonderful opportunity.

(Free translation)

Quechuan Glossary

Jatun Wasi	Great house.
Lantin	Radiant wrapping.
Pachamama	Nature. Universe.
Inti	Sun.
Intij Inti	Sun of Suns. Supreme cosmic energy.
Wasimasillay	Brother.
Janajpacha	Sky. Supreme reality.
Luluwen	(*Mapuche* term): subtle or material entity affecting those who sleep.
Chej-Pacha	Cosmic order.
Pahuichi	Typical forest dwelling.
Mancharisqa	Fearful and frightened.
Puchara	Sacred place.
K'uyuchiy	Rainbow.